LIFE AS AN EXPAT

FORTY-FIVE YEAR JOURNAL

AN OZARKS NATIVE

Any children of expatriates who reads this book can say, "so that is the story of my expat parents," because all expats who want to tell their story can basically change the character names in the book.

DONALD D. SHOCKLEY

Publishing Coordinator – Sharon Kizziah-Holmes
Book Design – Monica L. Holcomb

Indie Pub Press
Springfield, Missouri

ISBN -13: 978-1-970560-35-0 (B&W)
ISBN -13: 978-1-970560-34-3 (Color)

TABLE OF CONTENTS

ACKNOWLEDGMENTS

I am grateful to my wife who was patient and supportive of me when I needed it while I was away working, in my office shouting at someone on the phone, and later when writing this story. And, of course, I am grateful to all my children who probably needed their father many times while I was away working.

After I decided to write this story, I gathered information for each chapter, reviewing what should and should not be part of the story. As I reminisced while reading these reviews at each stage of my working life, I realized I owe a lot to all those who took responsibility to raise me. Although I lost my mother and father when I was eight years old, I often think about the love, care, and discipline they put into my life, and afterwards to my uncles and aunt, older brothers, sister, and their spouses who continued that love, care, and discipline. Therefore, although I might have disappointed all of them occasionally, I want to acknowledge the love and care they gave to me that should have made me a responsible father and person. Besides my mother and father, I would like to give a special acknowledgment to Uncle Joe and Aunt Mary Shockley; Maxine and her husband, Glen Replogle; Bill and his wife, Lorene Shockley; and Jim and his wife, Juanita Shockley. They all sacrificed their lives so we, the surviving younger children after our family tragedy in 1951, could grow up with equal opportunities in life. Some of them are already gone, but if I may modify a James Whitcomb Riley Poem for those very special people who are already just away:

I cannot say, and will not say
Some are dead. Some are just away.
With a cheery smile, and a wave of the hand,
They have wondered in an unknown land
And left us dreaming how very fair
It needs must be since they linger there.
And you-oh you, who the wildest yearn
For the old-time step, and the glad return,
Think of them as faring on as dear
In the love of there as the love as Here.
Think of them still the same. I say,
They are not dead – they are just away.

I had to rely on my three children for many of the stories and descriptions of our lives living as expatriates in another land as their memories are much fresher than mine. For reviewing, showing me mistakes, telling their stories, helping me write my stories in a more understandable manner, and mostly for recalling all those memories of the past I had forgotten, and Ben Beirens for the cover design, I am very grateful.

After writing a couple of books and struggling with getting them edited, I am grateful for the assistance of my cousin, Sally Lyons McAlear, who has published and edited several books as well as authored various publications. We learned through a former classmate who she met through a philanthropic educational Organization meeting a few years ago, that we were fourth cousins once removed. Since that time, I have become very close to Sally and her husband, John. She has worked tirelessly to help me with a family book and our past shared genealogy.

In this acknowledgement, I would also like to say thanks to all the great people I have worked with over the past fifty years or so, and especially to those who always gave their support to our company, Process Plant Services PPS, in the past thirty years while providing services to the gas, oil, petrochemical, and power plant industries. I could name many, but one of those people who had the nerve to question me when he felt I might be wrong, and then supported me in whatever decision I made, that was Mark D'Cruz.

A Special Note: I would also like to ask my family's forgiveness for being away when they probably needed me the most. This is my biggest regret in life. This book is for them!

PROLOGUE

A few years after retirement, my children ask me to write down information about all the places I worked and lived after going abroad in 1978. I semi-retired in 2007, fully retired in 2014, and I am still living outside of the USA in 2025, so that means I had to account for forty-seven years. I realized this would take some personal research for me since 1978, and to complicate it more, I have worked on six continents and had residence on five of those continents during this time span. After some thought about writing this for my children, I decided to make a journal that would be familiar to many expatriates around the world.

At eighty-two years old, this would be a task; the memory is not that good, and some records would be hard to find. So, I decided to give it a go, and maybe mix the records with some stories that are common to expatriates who have had similar careers. An expatriate is a person who lives or works outside his country of origin and plans to one day return to their country. The Association of Americans Resident Overseas (AARO) estimated there were 5.4 million Americans living abroad in 2025. I also decided to write this for all those expatriates who have similar stories, I am sure they can relate to most of the stories in this book, especially those who worked in the gas, oil, petrochemical, and power plant industries. We refer to expatriates simply as expats. Some names have been changed so there is no negative reflection on anyone who might have worked on projects with me.

For my first overseas project, I was fortunate to be contracted with a large engineering company that had been sending expatriates around the world to countries with various cultures and traditions. In 1978, M. W. Kellogg, now part of the Haliburton Corporation, was in the top three of the largest engineering and construction contractors in the world. An orientation was given to assist personnel to adjust to these countries for a smooth transition to cultural differences. We were expected to show respect, understand the laws, local customs, and sensitivity of the citizens of that country. We were especially given instructions on how to live in a strict Islamic country. Essential information for purchasing food and cooking in third-world countries is very important, especially those situated in hot climates. After a short time abroad, it became understandable where the term "Ugly American" came from when expatriates arrived often thinking they were special and better than locals. It doesn't take long for an expat to realize many people around the world are just as intelligent and often hold better values than we might possess.

One of my grandsons asked me if I had any incidents traveling that scared me and was my life ever seriously in danger. Everyone who has traveled to several countries over forty years would have a few stories, but I never felt my life in that much danger; well, maybe it was a couple of times. After mentioning several incidents that came to mind, he asked me which incident comes to mind first that could have been considered danger. You will find one of them in Chapter One.

Although traveling outside one's country for work, or career, for so many years can be very exciting, interesting, and rewarding, being away is not always nice for family and friends when you are possibly needed the most. Everyone has some regrets, and one of my main regrets in life is my being away often from my family, which has no doubt created unnecessary hardships. So, therefore, this book should not be considered a glamorous view of my personal life. It is simply forty-five years of an expat's life that hundreds of those who worked outside their home country can associate with similar working lives sitting lonely on a long airplane flight, feeling guilty while sleeping lonely in a strange hotel, in a work camp, company offices, or project facilities. So, most of us expatriates did not live a glamorous life travelling, and we usually can only say, "We have been there but didn't really do or see that." There is always a guilty feeling that all these years away was not really a career necessity but perhaps some selfishness, or it is partly due to one's personal attributes. One of my brothers once told me, "You were probably born under a wandering star." Maybe he was right. During my forty-five years working and living abroad.

CHAPTER 1

FIRST TRIP ABROAD & CATOOSA

After recovering from an on-the-job accident in the summer of 1978, at the age of thirty-five, I saw an advert in the St. Louis Post Dispatch for a millwright supervisor to work approximately four months in Indonesia. I thought I would consider it, as it was more money than I would make if I went back to work in Missouri on a power plant project, and I needed the money after being off for some time. Up to that point in my life, I had worked as a journeyman machinist until 1972, and after qualifying as a journey millwright, I worked on various types of projects that required my millwright experience. So, my journey began.

I was interviewed at a hotel near the St Louis airport by the company, M. W. Kellogg, a prominent engineering and construction firm specializing in petroleum and petrochemical industries headquartered in Houston Texas, currently referred to as Kellogg Brown, and Root, a division of Halliburton Company. I was offered the job based on passing an extensive physical and successfully receiving the proper vaccinations required for a visa and work permit. Fortunately, the doctor who gave me the physical examination was a Filipino who gave me some good advice on spending four months in a third-world country near the equator. He let me know that people native to these countries have a natural immunity that I would most likely not have against certain diseases, and he cautioned me to be careful and not to eat street food, and he gave me a paper on how to prepare vegetables. The company also gave an orientation on dos and don'ts in a foreign country, and what to take and not to take. One thing they stressed that I never forgot was that your passport is the most important document you have when out of your country; always keep it locked up in a safe place, and always keep a copy, I always keep a copy in my wallet. I was excited, but also, as it was my first trip abroad, I was also a little nervous. About a week after my physical and orientation, I flew to San Francisco to spend a day and night to get an Indonesian work visa, then flew on to Singapore on Pan American Airlines.

On arrival at the Changi Airport in Singapore, I was informed my luggage did not arrive and would arrive in about two to three days. I was met by a company representative who accompanied me to the Shangri La, a hotel in the center of Singapore. After the representative made a couple of phone calls, he told me I would have to remain in Singapore for up to three days until my luggage arrived. Apparently, if it was lost, I would have to buy clothes and necessary items before travelling on to Indonesia. After a long trip across the Pacific, I was excited but very tired, so the first evening I went to bed. The following day, the representative gave me Singapore dollars equivalent of twenty-five U.S. dollars a day for incidentals and was told my meals in the hotel were taken care of by my company. Even though Singapore in 1978 was a modern city, it was still a cultural awakening for me. Up to that time in my career, I had worked in several USA states in different industries but never outside the country.

I had two and a half days to spend and had no idea what to do, so I went to the lobby café in the hotel with a few brochures and a Coke trying to decide what I could do. A businessman sat down near me and started talking to me, asking what I was doing in Singapore. After explaining what I was doing there and my situation, he said he had some free time that day, and he offered to take me on a tour of Singapore. I agreed, and then he introduced himself to me. He handed me a business card, and to my surprise, he had the same last name as myself, Shockley. His card indicated he was from a Los Angeles jet engine repair company. In my company briefing, I was warned about possible scams, and my first thoughts were that this could be my first encounter abroad. He was in shock as well when I introduced myself. It soon came out that his father came from Belle, Missouri, and his grandfather was my great uncle, Albert Shockley. It turned out to be a great first day in a foreign land. He took me to all the Singapore tourist sites: Singapore Zoological Gardens; coffee in Raffles Hotel; lunch in Newton Circus, one of the famous Singapore hawker street food centers; cable car ride to Sentosa Island; a walk through China Town; a visit to the Central Fish Market at Jurong; and we ended the day shopping in areas on Orchard Road. The following day, I did all the shops on Orchard Road and surrounding areas, Lucky Plaza, and so on, with an evening of entertainment in an upper floor of Orchard Towers with Matthew Tan and the Mandarins, the Singapore Cowboy.

The following day, with my shopping done, basically a camera and plenty of 35mm film to take photos in Indonesia, a few gadgets, and with my recovered luggage, I boarded a short flight to Jakarta. Arriving at the airport around midday, I had my first real cultural shock with the airport guarded by the gun-toting army units in every part of the airport. Indonesia had a coup attempt in 1965 with the strongman General Sukarno appointed president for life. Indonesia was rather peaceful in 1978 but was ruled by an authoritarian government. After being met by the Kellogg representative in the late afternoon, I realized I was entering a third-world country. Singapore was different, but my cultural shock was beginning. My journey from the airport to just outside Cikempek was about forty miles due east of Jakarta. The project was about a mile out of the city. It was my first scary ride in Indonesia. I saw some accidents, crazy drivers thinking both sides of the road were OK, saw becaks (bike taxis) and rickshaws loaded with goods along canals where there were kids swimming, saw women washing clothes, and yes, a few were using the canals for a toilet. I arrived at the campsite for the project, Pupuk Kujang Fertilizer Plant, and was taken to a house, and given a maid who would assist me with cleaning, cooking, shopping, and washing clothes. It was just before 5:00 p.m., when I heard the local prayers from the mosque for the first time, a sound that became very familiar during my four-month stay. The housing built for the project was about a quarter mile from the plant. It had approximately fifty houses used by expatriates during construction and would later become permanent housing for plant employees and their families.

My company, M. W. Kellogg, was building an ammonia and urea plant. When I arrived, it was about 90% complete with commissioning and startup just beginning. I was hired to replace an older millwright supervisor who had to retire early due to health problems, and it was a critical stage of the project with approximately three to four months remaining. After a briefing with the site manager, I was introduced to the senior millwright supervisor, Des, my new boss. He was pleased to have some help, and I was happy I had a colleague with a lot of experience who was easy to work with as well. My first day wasn't very pleasant, though. Even with all amenities that came with the job. I came down with a very bad stomach problem that lasted for a couple of days.

I was well received by the Kellogg staff. They realized it was my first time working abroad, in fact, I soon became known by most of the staff as "Hayseed" or at times "Ozark Okie." An Oklahoma engineer on site gave me that name, and he said I was acceptable as the Ozarks boarders the state of Oklahoma. Other than degreed engineers, most of the expatriates there were former "oil patch" experienced persons from Texas, Oklahoma, or Louisiana. How could a hayseed from the Ozarks end up in that industry? Although I had worked in several different U.S. states in heavy industry, I had only worked in the oil and gas industry on a couple occasions.

With a day or two off occasionally, I did get the opportunity to visit Lake Jatiluhur, Purwakarta, Bandung, a drive through the beautiful mountains filled with rice paddies, and about a half mile walk down into a dormant volcano, while being carried most of the way by six Indonesians in a chair with pole handles. Staying in the camp was an experience for me, as there was always something going on. There were tennis and basketball courts, a small commissary for incidental groceries, a recreational room with a library, a nurse's office, and a small American school for company families who had children. In the evenings, there was always something going on. You would see an occasional local salesman selling ice cream shouting "Woody, Woody, Woody, and the children in the camp would gather for a local ice cream.

Occasionally, you would see someone who would be trying to sell hand-carved teak pieces, selling a monkey, a parrot in a cage, a six-foot snake tied to a pole carried by two Indonesians, or anything they felt an American would buy. At the end of the project, most animals were left in the camp. The job went well for me, and I learned a lot working with experienced expats and the Japanese whose company, Toyo, was responsible for the urea plant. I made some friends that I would work with in different areas of the world, and for many years thereafter and often would run across some of them in an international airport.

There are always stories to tell after a project abroad, but some are so bizarre no one would probably believe them. One story I tell my kids occasionally was how we received emergency blueprints. We would need these drawings from the Houston office, and if sent by courier, it would take two to three days. When an urgent drawing was required. one of us with technical knowledge had to be driven by a local driver about twenty miles into the mountains where a satellite-receiving station was located. Kellogg had a portable wire photo transmitter/receiver to send and receive urgent drawings via satellite. I went there a few times to sit for a simple drawing that would take about two hours to send or receive. You could hear the "click, click, click of the needle on the drum until we had a readable printed drawing, and even then, we could barely read it. We would have been shocked to know thirty years later, we would be able to receive a very good blueprint with an iPhone in just a few minutes.

One story that amazed me happened one night when our plant had to shut down due to no cooling water. An ammonia plant requires an enormous amount of water for cooling, and if the water flow stops, the plant shuts down. A night plant operator and I drove about five miles upriver to find the river had silted up on a bend of the river about a quarter of mile upstream from our cooling water pumps due to very heavy rain. The pumps shut down automatically when the water level reached a low level. When I saw it, I thought it would take a month to clear it up and get the plant running again. My thoughts were that I would spend more than the autumn in Indonesia. The river at that point was about thirty yards across, and the water was spilling over into a rice paddy. My operations colleague, who had been on the project for about six months, said we would come back tomorrow while it was being cleared. The next evening when we arrived, there were a couple hundred Indonesians standing in the muddy river, each with a board drawing mud out of the river from one to another until it was on the riverbank. By the time Kellogg had time to get a couple of large diggers on site, the job was almost done, with most of the silt removed. We were able to start up the pumps in just three days. My operator colleague laughed at me; I was totally in shock. I was sure it would take a few weeks to clear up the river with our large equipment including what I thought would include a mechanical digger on a barge. He knew the Indonesians would come through! That was one of my experiences that let me know what an exceptional people these Indonesians were in an emergency.

My first project abroad was a learning experience on how not to fall into the typical traps the first time as expatriates abroad often fall into. It was my opinion that everyone has regrets, and I must admit I have regrets, and some of them are a few judgement decisions I made while on that project. Some of these regrets falls under the old cliché "what happened there stays there." One story that I will tell, however, happened one night just after midnight. When the plant startup began, I was put on night shift with a local crew for any equipment problems; we had to keep the plant running. The plant startup operators were on rotating shifts with one group supposed to be sleeping. An attribute of many expatriates abroad is drinking heavily when off work, but fortunately, this was never one of my temptations. That morning around 1:00 am, I happened to see a pickup truck coming out of the camp headed around the site with what I knew must be someone drunk and probably headed out of the project into town. The driver had run off the road, so I went over and helped get the truck out of the ditch. I asked where he was going, and after he said he was going into town to buy cigarettes, I reminded him we were not supposed to ever drive outside the project boundaries, but he insisted he was going anyway. After trying to convince him otherwise, I agreed to ride with him to the security gate, and, if the guards would let him go, I would get out of the truck. If not, he would drive back to his room. I never thought the guards would let him through. When he got to the gate, he accelerated threw the gate and turned onto the main road hitting a becak with a woman passenger. There were always people on the road for twenty-four hours. The big problem was that there was also a police truck just outside the gate that saw the accident, and in an Islamic country, if she had been killed, the driver would be stoned. We were immediately taken to a local jail, or a place where they locked up those who had broken the law. It was not nice being in the dark with possible criminals. After a couple of hours, the driver, who I call J.J. had passed out as the police took us back to the security guards. They stopped to let the guards know they were taking us to another location. Fortunately for us, one of the guards was related to the head of police in Cikempek and intervened for us. First, we were fortunate that the lady was not hurt badly, and finally the situation was settled within an hour or so at my house by emptying my refrigerator, providing a few gifts, plus $200.00 dollars cash. I was also relieved that morning when the security guard explained to the project manager that I had tried to convince JJ not to drive. I kept my job with a warning, and J.J. was sent home. Lesson learned for that misjudgment; however, like all first timers, there were a few more to come. Some I will talk about, and some come under that old cliché, "what happened there stays there."

By mid-November 1978, after my four months was up, and the plant had started up and was considered ready for test run, I felt like a veteran; however, I was still known as "Hay Seed" until the day I left site. Sorry, there are no personal or site photos in Chapter One. I took about twenty rolls of 35mm pictures, but I decided to wait to get them developed in the USA when I was home only to find out the camera, I bought in Singapore was damaged.

Just before I left the project, the site manager let me know he arranged for me to become a permanent employee as I had been hired for that project on a temporary basis. After arriving home and a few weeks off work, I was assigned to the Kellogg office in Houston to assist with gathering of materials for my next project that was to be in Catoosa, Oklahoma, the last project for me on American soil. I rented my house in Warrenton, Missouri. Kellogg moved my family with everything I owned to Tulsa, Oklahoma, about five miles from the Catoosa Nitric Acid Process Plant. My children had to adjust to another school in the middle of a school year, something that would be common to them in the future, often leaving new friends they would never see again. What initially seemed to be an unfortunate Christmas turned out positively, as the children enjoyed their stay at the hotel while we waited for our rented house to become available after the new year. It was a small nine-month project with approximately fifteen Kellogg staff monitoring a local contractor that was building the plant. Most of the staff were engineers who were assigned to the project as an interim job as they had become "Veteran Expatriates" who preferred to work abroad, so it was another opportunity to learn about life working as an expatriate listening to their stories. I realized to make the best of my career in that industry, I needed to have more education for advancement. While from June to mid-November 1979 working in Catoosa from, I started a correspondence course in engineering management. With a family, I couldn't stop working to go to college, so I decided I could eventually achieve an engineering degree or at least an associate's degree.

After my first trip abroad, I learned many of the dos and don'ts of an expat abroad. It didn't take long to understand the difference in electrical currency, even though I was told in my orientation before mobilizing to Indonesia, I still had to learn the hard way at times. I had taken a few items that were electrical, which were one hundred twenty volts and sixty hertz I thought would work with a convertor I bought in Singapore. The converter did change the voltage, and my clock didn't keep good time, it was for a different hertz current. I also learned to take a short-wave radio to get up to date news on Voice of America and the BBC short waves. I eventually bought a short-wave radio, with a voltage converter, that could pick up both programs from anywhere in the world. An expat abroad learns from one another and depends on each other for many different reasons, especially culture mistakes that can be embarrassing and sometimes considered rude to residents.

CHAPTER 2

TRINIDAD

Approximately a month prior to finishing the contract at Catoosa, I received a notice for my next assignment to start on December 1979 get all the documentation needed for a work visa in Trinidad. I wasn't sure where that was exactly; I only knew it was off the coast of Venezuela in the Caribbean Sea, and English was the national language. It was a family status job for about two years to build a fertilizer complex made up of two ammonia and urea plants. So, we were about to move to a foreign country as a family with three children under twelve years old, which meant a lot of planning and deciding what to take with the weight allowance and suggestions of the company. A Caribbean country with a lot of beaches in a tropical climate. That sounded very exciting! The contract was expected to last around two years, with a week's rest & relaxation (R&R) leave after six months for the family somewhere nearby in the Caribbean and a two-week home leave after twelve months for the family.

The company was to provide transportation to and from work, a furnished apartment, and grade school for the children. After an orientation on moving to Trinidad, we packed up what was recommended into twelve large cases and trunks and flew to Trinidad. The project was in the Point Lisas Industrial area of Couva, and the furnished apartment was in Port of Spain, about thirty miles or less with transportation provided by the company. Upon arrival, we were provided hotel accommodations in the "Upside down" Hilton Hotel near Queens's Park Savannah. The lobby, conference room, restaurant, hotel shop, and swimming pool were located on the top floor with all the guest rooms under. The hotel was situated on the side of a hill overlooking the beautiful Savannah. We were initially to move in our apartment in Diego Martin just outside Port of Spain, within a week, however, due to delays, we stayed in two large hotel rooms for over six weeks. Boy did the children like that, swimming every day after school and weekends. However, as a family just a few days in a hotel gets tiring very quickly. And the children never forgot another Christmas in a hotel. They got accustomed to the pastries at teatime in the hotel, and at Christmas, it was even more special. The kids had to get used to it. A new expatriate life journey was just beginning, nothing like a drive through the "Robinson's Neighborhood" on the way to school!

The project included two ammonia plants that had been relocated to Trinidad after projects were cancelled, so erecting of equipment that had been in storage was a challenge. Driving to and from the work site about forty miles six days a week was also a challenge. The main road was two lanes and very busy. Several of the expats were involved in road accidents including two who lost their lives. Another culture shock was crossing a river about halfway to the site. Just beside the bridge was a location where the Trinidadian Indian population held their almost daily burial ceremonies, which included burning the bodies. From the bridge, we could see the fire and a terrible smell in the air. Trinidad was made up of forty-five percent Indians, mostly Hindu, forty-five African race; and ten percent others. Once again, I was fortunate to have the experience of a Millwright Supervisor who was my immediate boss.

The project had some delays due to missing parts, and many pieces of the equipment needed replacement or repair on site before installation due to poor preservation in former locations, which made the job very interesting for me as a former machinist. We did a lot of on-site machining of equipment, pipe flanges, vessels, and many other pieces of equipment. With the delays and some local labor problems, Kellogg sent one of their top project directors, Bill N, to assist the site manager. There were several external problems as well as some situations with constructing a plant with equipment refurbishment on site. Each morning, Bill N walked around the site in his aluminum hard hat, moving quickly and without concentrating on any single task. However, at the daily meeting, he seemed to know everything about the status of every part of the project. Aluminum hard hats were illegal, but he was the boss. I mention Bill N as I credit him for keeping me from getting fired and saving my career with Kellogg. After going through a period of anger problems, he called me into his office and told me if I continued to lose my temper, I would not only get fired, but I could expect a heart attack; he had already had two himself. Throughout the remainder of the project, I began to admire and respect Bill N. The day I left the site, he called me into his office, and the man of few words only said, "You will work for me again," and I did, on two more major projects.

It was a tough job, but I gained a lot of experience and made many more new friends I would work with over the next twenty-five years or so. For a family of five, it really was a dream job. Although we worked six days a week, Sundays and local holidays were a great opportunity to see and enjoy the sights, and we enjoyed a complete week off during two carnivals. Trinidad is well known for its carnivals. The country and all businesses on the entire island except essentials and emergency units, went into party mode. All day and night, there were steel pan drum bands and Calypso groups competing on stages in the Queen Savannah Park in Port of Spain and all other city parks twenty-four hours a day. The last day of the carnival ended with a huge parade of decorated floats and an endless number of trailers loaded with steel pan bands playing their music. The steel pan drums were made from the bottom half or quarter with the bottom pounded in sections to make a certain musical note. I am not sure if it is true or not, but I was told crime went down during carnival week as the criminals also took off to party. I am also sure the rum breweries probably sold more in that week than the remainder of the year, and, of course, there were many headaches and hangovers thereafter for a few days. I will just walk down memory lane with a few of the other sites in Trinidad our family enjoyed while there with a few short paragraphs.

Trinidad and Tobago has many natural beautiful beaches. We would visit different beaches on Sundays or any other day when off work and out of school. Tobago has an exceptional beach that we visited a few times. The depth of the water is only about three feet with white silky sand perfect for snorkeling and swimming for a family. Tobago is an island about ten miles North of Trinidad and at that time a fifteen-minute flight on an inexpensive local airplane was the best way to get there.

On the east coast of Trinidad, we had the opportunity to visit Matura Beach where thousands of large sea turtles travel thousands of miles each year to lay their eggs. We took part in helping preserve nature during the hatching of their eggs. The newly hatched baby turtles had to scramble to the water to avoid birds and other species grabbing them for a quick meal. So, we all joined in to hand carry as many as possible once hatched to the water's edge where they were then on their own with dangers awaiting them in the ocean. Another threat to these turtles each year was locals who loved to build a little fire and cook a large turtle turned upside down, which I am sure brought very tasty meat and soup. This was a fun day for the family along with enjoying the beach as well as saving a few baby turtles.

There were two beaches we considered equally our favorite, Maracas Bay and Chaguaramas. Chaguaramas was great for just swimming and lying on the beach and was a little closer to our apartment. And the other, Maracas Bay was great for surfing, lying on the beach, and there were several food stalls. Chaguaramas was a former submarine base for the U.S. Navy during, and a few years later, the water became deep very quickly from the shore and there was a nice platform about ten feet above the sea in high tide. All our children became excellent swimmers and even enjoyed diving from that platform. One thing there that was considered a threat was there was always the possibly of a shark swimming in the bay. We never saw one and never heard of anyone getting bitten by a shark, but many times, we would hear a whistle from a lifeguard announcing a possible shark citing, which usually turned out to be a school of curious dolphins. Until they get up close, it's hard to tell.

Maracas Bay was much larger and had perfect shape for somebody surfing and swimming, as well as food stalls where we could never miss one of those famous shark sandwiches. We all would rent a surfboard and try to catch a wave coming just in time for it to carry us for about one hundred yards to the beach.

Debbie was eleven years old, Rich was ten years old, and Tammy was eight years old. It didn't take long before we knew just when to start paddling on the board to catch the wave just at the right moment for a good surfing. Maracas Bay was about fifteen miles by a double-lined road through the mountains, and in Trinidad at that time, caution driving was always a must. One of my colleagues, Ron Everett, and I decided we would hike from the apartment with his son, which we did but found out it was much more of a task than we envisioned. The following day at work, there were two guys limping around the project with sore legs, with Ron's son Troy not feeling any pain. There was a famous walk from the east side of the bay that ended up at a large waterfall with a large pool to swim in. It was about ten miles through the mountain trails. We did this walk several times, and when a colleague, Mike, from Louisiana, heard there were large crawfish, he always had enough to keep his wife, Jenny, happy as well, they missed their crawfish étouffée and crawfish boil. They lived next door, and we could always smell those delicious pots on her stove.

There were other interesting places of interest we would visit on occasions. A couple included visits made to the wetlands to see a yearly gathering of thousands of scarlet ibis on a bird-watching boat tour in Caroni Swamp and a visit to an old cocoa and coffee estate where we watched the beans being smashed under feet as locals danced and sang old folk songs. We also visited La Brea Pitch Lake where it is said Colombus had his ships repaired using the thick tar from the lake. While visiting Pitch Lake, Richie, our son, decided to climb up one of the tall coconut trees. He wanted to pick one of the coconuts; however, as he was about to pull one off, a swarm of bees began to sting him. He was about twenty feet off the ground, and we were afraid he would jump, which would have been disastrous. We all began to shout, "don't jump climb down." Fortunately, he kept cool until he was close to the ground and then safely jumped. He was a little sore and swollen from the bee stings, but he was OK.

One holiday while off work, a local man from the project invited four of us to go offshore fishing in his boat. He suggested it would be nice to take my son, Richie. The boat was a large old cabin cruiser with an inboard motor, and he assured us it was in good shape, so we went about five miles offshore and tied up to an old oil rig platform where he said was a great place to catch fish. It was, and we were catching fish for about two hours when an unexpected storm came up. It began rocking the boat roughly, so we had to stop fishing, and the owner decided it was best to go ashore as soon as the storm dissipated. After a while, it calmed down some and he tried to start the motor, but it wouldn't start, and the storm came back up with high waves. It became a little scary with only three life jackets and no way to communicate for help to anyone on land. We were all scared, including the boat owner, as the waves were beginning to beat the boat up to the platform. There were only two ropes, and one was tying the boat to the platform, so the owner suggested to tie one around Richie, who had a life jacket, and position him as high up on the platform as possible in case the boat sank. We were sure it was the end for us, but after a few hours, the storm calmed down, and the owner finally got the boat running. We made it back to shore safely after dark, feeling foolish and lucky. I think that was another good lesson I learned, I can't imagine today going out on an old boat on the open sea without life jackets for everyone.

Our TV stations in Trinidad had several channels, mainly Trinidad programs and a few U. S. replayed programs. We got our news mostly from a BBC television channel. There were always Trinidadian entertainment programs such as calypso, soca, chutney, and steelpan music, each with unique cultural roots and influences. There was calypso music on every day, and especially around the carnival period. Of course, you could be sure the number one calypso singer, The Mighty Sparrow, would be on radio and television all through the day. Another calypso song that was played often, what we know as, "Working for the Yankee Dollar", a phrase famously featured in the song "Rum and Coca-Cola". It became a major hit in the 1940s, particularly popularized by The Andrews Sisters in 1944. The original version of "Rum and Coca-Cola" lamented that U.S. soldiers were debauching local women who "saw that the Yankees treat them nice and they give them a better price." The final stanza described a newlywed couple whose marriage is ruined when "the bride run away with a soldier lad and the stupid husband went staring mad." By the time we left Trinidad, we were well versed in some of the local calypso songs, fans of the steel bands, and impressed with the unique Trinidad culture.

The project had come to an end in October 1981, and we were repatriated back to the USA. We, like all expatriates, bought local carvings, souvenirs, and any other thing we thought we could hang on our walls once settled in the USA, which usually end up later in storage or somewhere in the basement. Kellogg told me there wasn't another project for a little while, so I went home on standby until something else would come up requiring my services. When we left Catoosa, we sold our house in Missouri, so we had our things shipped to Bartow, Florida, where we bought a house and where the kids could go to school. The children were thirteen, twelve, and ten years old when we left Trinidad. After a few weeks, I was asked if I was interested in taking a two-year contract on a large aluminum bauxite project in Venezuela on loan, there were a few Kellogg members on the project. This type of project was something a little different from Kellogg's services, but it had a large amount of rotating equipment I was familiar with. I agreed and after a quick trip to Puerto Ordaz, Venezuela, for an interview with the Alusuisse Aluminum from Zurich, Switzerland, we began to pack for the next adventure.

Chapter 3

Venezuela

I had a project orientation over the phone; we were to mobilize to Venezuela in December 1981. We had my notes to prepare for mobilizing to Venezuela. I was told we would be provided with a three-bedroom furnished mobile home on a campsite with a clubhouse and tennis courts fenced in with twenty-four-hour security. My notes didn't say what was furnished, so we packed pots, pans, dishes, towels, sheets, and anything needed for a household other than furniture. We were allowed a small container of items but were told to take everything else we needed as extra luggage and the company would pay, so we had thirteen pieces of luggage, trunks, and cases (large ones.) When we were met at the airport in Puerto Ordas, the company representative came with a car and pickup but was shocked when he saw what we had as "extra luggage." Fortunately, the camp had a place to store our extra shipment until we could move into our mobile home. For two weeks, we were put up in the beautiful Intercontinental Hotel, Ciudad Guayana, just below Llovizna Falls (la llovizna, The

Drizzle). Richie and Tammy found plenty to do, playing in the nice nature park and watching the monkeys in the trees. However, Richie and Tammie took advantage of the loose sticks and leaves in the park to make their own manger scene near the hotel This was the third Christmas we had spent in a hotel; the hotel did have several events for the residents. However, Richie and Tammie took advantage of the loose sticks and leaves in the park to make their own manger scene near the hotel.

Richie and Tammie also had a little fun with the popular Menudo, a popular Puerto Rican boy band who were staying in the hotel. The following is Tammy's description of how they tried to get audiences, and, of course, autographs, with Menudo. "We noticed on one day that there were crowds of people hanging out in the lobby and outside. We asked the staff (by then we were familiar with the hotel staff, and which ones spoke English) what was going on. They told us the popular singing band called "Menudo" was staying in the hotel. They said they were told that the singers would come down shortly to greet fans. There were crowds waiting to see the singers. Richie and I found out what floor they were staying on. So, we would go up the stairs to their floor and push the button for the elevator. Then we would ride down to the lobby, and we could hear all the people cheering (because they could see the elevator had stopped on their floor). Then the elevator doors opened in the lobby, and they would see Richie and me. Rather than local fans cheering, all of them would say "awwwww" in disappointment!! Sooooo, we would go do it again!!! And again!!! And again!!!!! They soon got very tired of seeing us." Fortunately, our mobile home was ready, and we were able to move out of the hotel before we were thrown out!

The camp was very nice, but with all we had brought,

which we didn't need most of it, the mobile home was cramped until we sold or gave away some of our personal things and built a few storage cabinets in each bedroom. Puerto Ordaz is a city in the Bolivar state in the southeastern part of Venezuela at the point where Orinoco and Caroni rivers join about one hundred fifty miles before draining into the Atlantic Ocean. It has a population of around one hundred thousand people with several shops and restaurants. San Felix, a much larger city across the Caroni River, was less developed, and had about twice the population as Puerto Ordaz. Up the Orinoco River was Ciudad Bolivar, the capital of the Venezuela's Bolívar state, a very beautiful part of the country.

On Monday morning after arrival, I was picked up from the hotel with a new pickup truck, which became my transportation, and then taken to the job to meet the project staff site manager and my boss, Mr. Chamberlian. He was another Kellogg employee who had been assigned to the project. After explaining the project and my responsibilities, I was taken on a tour of the project. It was something again new to me and a very large project. It didn't take long for me to figure out that all the field supervisors and contractors didn't like the idea of me (and the position I was hired for). The project, a bauxite separation plant, was a large project that included a lot of rotating equipment, pumps, compressors, turbines, conveyers, power plants, and so on. It was to supply a Reynolds Aluminum plant close by and their plants in the USA with bauxite to make aluminum ingots. Mr. Chamberlain was having a difficult time with his staff and keeping all the mechanical contractors installing equipment to some sort of standard. In fact, they had none. I was hired to write rotating equipment standards and then to assure all equipment would be installed to that standard. It was a huge challenge for me, but I had Kellogg procedures and standards to work with, although there was a lot of equipment not used in the gas and oil industry.

My first few months were very stressful, and at times felt like going home, but gradually, I became accepted with the assistance of a mechanical contractor that had worked on a Kellogg project in western Venezuela on their past project, so they were familiar with the standards and procedures I was instituting with the backing of Mr. Chamberlain. The project went well for me, and I learned a lot working with different nationalities. It being a Swiss company, there was about forty percent of the management staff being Swiss. It was mixed with British, Australian, German, and about twenty percent Americans.

The second scary incident happened during a Friday evening when I was invited out to eat by the site engineering manager. We went to one of the best restaurants in Puerto Ordaz. Just as we were leaving, a police force entered the restaurant looking for a Columbian gang who had just robbed a payroll truck. The gang were in the restaurant enjoying the fruit from their robbery. The police all had rifles and ordered the gang to leave the restaurant and get on a bus outside. After loading them, the police came back in and ordered remaining people to present their identification. Like all the rest, I took mine out to present, but the policeman poked me in the ribs and ordered me to get on the bus. I said, "I am not with them," which immediately resulted in another poke, which bruised my ribs; so taking the advice of my colleague, I got on the bus. He said, "don't worry", he would get me out in an hour or so. Once at the police station after going through a long line with the Columbians, but once at the desk, the receiving policeman tore up my Venezuelan papers saying, "You don't have the proper papers." I spent two days in that cell, a room of about twenty-foot square with a place to relieve oneself and a water faucet to get a drink. I and a young German, who was about six-foot-four, and I sat together for protection. I spent two full nights and days until my company found me. I had been taken to an unexpected jail and registered under my middle name. I was released after my company was advised to look under all my names, and without any problems other than smelling very bad and bruised ribs.

The assignment was a dream for the family, so I will finish this chapter with some memories of about two years of life in the beautiful country of Venezuela. The school year had begun, so the kids were off to school the next Monday after arriving with an international school provided by the company, grades one to eight. It was well set up with two teachers, a couple, Mr. and Mrs. Greeney. Debbie needed to finish her year in the United States, so she joined after finishing the semester of school. Her Aunt Vickie and Uncle Bob gave her boarding while finishing her semester in 1982. Debbie, Richie and Tammie had a special relation with their aunt. It was the second school the kids attended outside the United States. We were very pleased with the school, and the Greeneys; Mr. Greeney was a special character, but both he and his wife spent extra time with all students who might need extra attention. One memory of Mr. Greeney was that he only used green in all his writing.

There was plenty for the family to do in the south part of Venezuela, especially since the Caroni and Orinoco rivers came together just past Puerto Ordaz. On the Caroni, there were places to swim safely with very clear water and cool in hot weather. We also did a little sifting for diamonds and other precious stones. With had a set of three Saruca screens, which were designed to classify material and concentrate heavy minerals like diamonds. We were very fortunate during our stay in Venezuela to fill a coffee can about half full of diamonds. However, they were all industrial grade, not beautiful jewelry-grade diamonds. A five-gallon container full of the diamonds we found would bring about ten dollars. However, we did enjoy sifting for them.

A weekend barbeque on the Caroni River was fantastic and included a little fishing. We were able to catch many fish, a few we didn't know what they were, but some were special. One that we caught often, and it was very tasty, was called Payara, a carnivorous fish, with its head having a particular dentition (arrangement of teeth), which gave it the nickname of a vampire fish. Another well-known, and some people consider them dangerous in certain situations, was Piranha. They have a body like a perch but have strong jaws equipped with sharp, triangular teeth. The ones we caught were around six to ten inches, and occasionally one a little larger. They are often perceived as ferocious predators, but their diet is mostly omnivorous. They consume a mix of fish, snails, aquatic plants, and even fruits. While they can exhibit aggressive feeding behavior, especially in groups, attacks on larger animals or humans are rare. When we had caught another type of fish, you needed to reel it in a hurry, or your line would suddenly pull down and leave your hook with only a head and a few bones. When they see another fish or animal struggling in the water, hundreds of these Piranhas would attack. They were also very tasty. I often fished with a Venezuelan, Adam Brown. His father was an Englishman and mother Venezuelan, but he grew up around Puerto Ordaz and knew where the fish were plentiful. He was a special person, but he didn't like to lose fishing tackles, so when our lines got hung up underwater, he would jump off the boat and, in a few minutes, come up with tackle intact. He said those Piranhas would not attack unless you had a wound or were struggling. I decided to let Adam take care of my underwater tackle when tangled up below. I was able to fish in the Orinoco River and caught as many fish as we wanted, including a stingray that surprised me. There were a few saltwater fish and dolphins as far inland as Puerto Ordaz from the sea.

The rivers offered many unspoiled natural attractions in 1982. We often went as far as up the river from Puerto Ordaz as the roads would allow, and then at times, we would take a boat or hike. We took advantage of a flight from Puerto Ordaz on an old DC3 aircraft to circle in and out of the basin of Angel Falls. The pilot would fly the airplane into the falls leaning the plane one way so the people on the left would see and take a few pictures, then fly in a different direction so the people on the right side of the plane could see and take their pictures. Angel Falls is just over four hundred miles upriver from Puerto Ordaz. On another occasion, we flew just under Angel Falls and visited an indigenous Indian camp. Of course it was set up for tourists like us, but it was very interesting. We were told once about a Indian burial site east of Puerto Ordaz about twenty-five miles where we could dig up pottery and other artifacts. We did this a few times until we were finally told to stop as it was consecrated, and looking back from the present, I am ashamed we dug up some of those pieces. What we took from that site were handles of pottery containers, which we still have in our basement or somewhere in storage. We should never have touched or dug up any of these artifacts.

There were all those special side-of-the-road food outlets with a few "tasties" we could never pass up. The arepa is one of the oldest dishes in South America. They were available only on the street or road. The arepa consists of two pieces of bread made with corn flour and filled with different ingredients. Most of the time it was filled with local cheese or sausage. Then there was the Cachapa, made of fresh corn, butter, and a few other simple ingredients, and then filled with melted cheese or meat. They were essentially stuffed corn pancakes. There were several local restaurants with local food, and one of our favorites was an Italian restaurant that had a huge wood fired oven in the middle of the restaurant where the cook was continuously shoveling pizzas in and out with his long wooden shovel. The food was delicious, but the ambiance was equally amazing for an evening out with the family.

Life there was very good period; I enjoyed the project and felt it was good for the family and added an experience that was new to my career. There are many more memories we could put in this book, but I think I need to keep this short as there are a few more projects and countries to cover. I am sure my children could add many stories from that period.

CHAPTER 4

ONE AND HALF YEARS
ON SHORT TERM PROJECTS

After returning from Venezuela at the end of January 1983, we had our household storage moved to Bartow, Florida, where we bought a house after our Trinidad project. Debbie was beginning her second year of high school, Richie began his first year, and Tammy was in the sixth grade. We felt it was better for all the children to finish their school in the U.S.A. In December, Kellogg asked me to take a short-term single status assignment on a Liquid Natural Gas (LNG) plant revamp on Das Island, United Emirates in the Persian Gulf around the middle of February 1983 as a site superintendent over crafts. After arriving back to Florida at the end of January, we were pressed to settle in our house and get the children in school in Bartow as well as me preparing to mobilize to Indonesia. In just fifteen days. However, I felt this new experience would be good for my resume even if I would decide to remain in the U.S.A. after the assignment. I accepted the offer and mobilized the middle of February to Abu Dhabi for orientation. It was my first time in the Middle East and another cultural shock. I had to stay in Abu Dhabi for two days, so I took advantage of the time to look around at the local surroundings where I could walk or take a short taxi ride. I enjoyed the souks (Market places) and a camel race just outside the city. Earlier in my life, I had become obsessed with the history of the Middle East, so this was a great opportunity for me to be there and to get an understanding of the people. I had become accustomed to "a call to prayer from the mosques" while in Indonesia but observing the keffiyeh (head covering for men) and thobes (robes wore by Arabic men) was a new cultural awakening.

On the third day in the Persian Gulf area, I flew on a small airplane from Abu Dhabi to a small landing strip on Das Island. The island is about a quarter mile in width and three-quarters of a mile in length. The airstrip was at an angle between the plant and the campsite. It was almost impossible for a large airplane to land. However, just a month before I arrived, an Iranian fighter jet pilot had landed against the flight tower refusing his landing, and the strip was supposed to be too short. He landed anyway, and fortunately, with a dangerous LNG (liquid natural gas) plant running, he landed safely. He was seeking asylum. As I landed, a large ferry boat landed and around four hundred Indians debarked, they were craftsmen who had been hired to carry out the revamp activities. They were taken to their living quarters for the expected four-month revamp activities. Little did I know the next day a colleague and I would have to gather these four hundred men for an orientation we jointly had to deliver before they were to begin work. Fortunately, my colleague had experience working with Indians, so he did his bit first. As he began laying out the rules and safety requirements, I saw four hundred heads bobbing back and forth to show their agreement, which was another cultural shock, and for some reason, it struck me as funny. My colleague saw me laughing and afterwards used a few bad words to let me know he wasn't pleased. I was next, but I did get through it and found out during the project these craftsmen were very skilled and friendly.

The project went well although we worked twelve hours a day seven days a week. I didn't mind working that many hours a day with twelve hours off at night. There was a recreation room, a bar, and a camp mess hall run by the famous catering Spenny's Group that provided camp mess halls throughout the Middle East gas and oil projects. So, the food was great; we even had to wear nice clean clothes and had candle lights sitting on each table on one night of the week. Most evenings, my colleagues would go to the bar and drink and play games until it closed at 9 p.m. It was my first LNG plant, so I took the opportunity to go to my room in the evenings to study and learn the process of LNG from the plant operation manuals.

The project was on schedule, and I was enjoying the job, but in mid-March, an emergency message came to the site from the Kellogg Houston office for me. The only message was for me to immediately mobilize home ASAP as my daughter had been kidnapped. So, I rushed off the island and flew to Tampa, Florida, worried about my daughter. However, when I arrived home in Bartow, I found out my daughter, Debbie, and three friends had taken our second car, a Ford Pinto, and drove to Los Angeles, California. Debbie was always a respectful daughter but was sort of a rebel. It turned out she had two girlfriends, and one girl's boyfriend had talked her into driving them to California. When they arrived in Los Angeles, the police randomly stopped the car and found the boy had drugs on him. All were arrested and taken to jail. When I found out where they were, I called my nephew who lived in Los Angeles, and he got a very scared girl released from jail without any charges. She said the police checked every hole on her body for drugs. That left me with a Pinto with a bad water pump and four bad tires to pick up my daughter and drive all the way across the lower part of the United States back to Bartow, Florida. You can imagine a three-long-day drive back to Florida after I got the car repaired. For three days during the trip, I didn't talk to Debbie until we arrived at the city limits of Bartow, and then started talking to her. I told her I felt she had learned her lesson and expected her to realized what she had done, and I would never scold her any more thereafter, and I didn't. A lesson learned for both of us. With the salary I lost and other costs, I figured it cost me seventeen thousand dollars.

Kellogg said the project was basically at a point where it could be finished with the personnel on the projects. I really hated to let Kellogg know she hadn't been kidnapped. I remained home for a month before taking another project. Well, I thought Debbie and I learned a lesson, but it seems she was the only one who learned. I accepted another single status assignment in Indonesia, which was to be six to nine months starting in Mid-May 1983. It was on a major LNG plant revamp after running for several years without being shut down. The project was located near the town of Bontang, an eastern costal town in East Kalimantan, formerly called Borneo. My position was to be a rotation equipment specialist's supervisor. The plant had been built by the Bethel Corporation, but the process was a Kellogg design. The project was owned and run by P.T. Badak of Indonesia that consisted of the two LNG trains that were being revamped one at a time while two new trains were in the process of being built.

So, I mobilized again through Singapore with a short flight on to Balikpapan, Kalimantan, just south of the equator about twenty miles. From Balikpapan, I boarded a small airplane that had a capacity of sixteen people and a few site supplies. The flight would take about fifteen minutes to fly over the equator, but as we taxied down the runway, a call came from the tower instructing the airplane to return to the terminal. The P.T. Badak operations manager was on the flight. As we arrived, he was told there had been a major explosion in one of the LNG trains killing many people and the plant was on fire. What an arrival for my new project! But after a couple hours, we were given the go ahead to fly on to the site. One of the tower vessels was over pressured causing the explosion, killing seven people, injuring several others, and with several of local construction personnel uncounted for, some had run into the jungle. It took several hours to put out the fire and account for all personnel on site. It was a major setback for the site.

My duties and position changed the following day. The B-Train was to be fast tracked to get it producing LNG as soon as possible. I was assigned to the compressor deck to work directly under the P.T. Badak rotating engineer to oversee the revamp of the three large compressors liaising with General Electric turbine and Clark compressor company representatives for the completion of the overhauls of the equipment. It was another new experience for me working ten hours a day, six days a week. The camp housed nearly two thousand people with single status and family housing, I had a room in the single status section. The camp was first class with a mess hall where one could choose Indonesian or American food. There were several recreation rooms, bars, tennis courts, basketball court, grocery store, and a dock with many sail and fishing boats. I worked hard and enjoyed my job and fishing on my weekly days off and running each evening in the jungle after work. There were several British men on the site who had started a running game on days off called "Hash House

Harriers," which was supposedly originally started in Malaysia by the British soldiers during imprisonment by the Japanese during World War II. It was about a two-mile run with false trails, which were designed so the fast runners and slow runners would end the race at about the same time. The fast runners often took the false trail that slowed them down and slower runners realized they were false, so everyone usually finished around the same time. The trails were laid out earlier in the day by shredded paper.

I took a two-week home leave rather than a four-month rest and relaxation holiday, which was a week in the nearby area of Indonesia, such as Bali. I paid the difference as I felt I needed to go home to the family. I finish my duties by end of November 1983, which was nice as I could have Christmas at home before taking another assignment.

In early January of 1984, Kellogg asked me to take "another single status assignment" of three to four months to assist the on-site rotating engineer and train the client's mechanical personnel. I mobilized on the first of February 1985. It was an ammonia / urea plant like the first project I had in Java and Trinidad on my first and second jobs abroad, and it was owned by the same client, Pupuk Indonesia, the same owner in Java where I had worked on my first project abroad. It was a project that had been stopped and mothballed when it was about ninety percent completed by another contractor, but the ammonia plant was a Kellogg design, which I was familiar with the equipment. Kellogg was contracted to finish and start up the project including training of local personnel. The location was twelve miles north of Bontang, which was only accessible by a small road from Bontang, a helicopter pad, and by boat. Bontang was a fishing village prior to the LNG plant projects with most buildings built on stilts in the sea. There were also a couple of islands near Bontang with small villages consisting of several stilt houses and a small grocery store. It also had a very nice camp but very small compared to the Bontang project.

The project went well, and I finished mid-April 1984. We weren't pleased with the school system in Bartow and decided to move to Missouri and buy a house. After buying the house in Marshfield, Missouri, we moved the family after their school year finished in early June that year.

CHAPTER 5

BONTANG

In Mid-May 1984, I was offered a plant maintenance supervisor position for Roy M. Huffington on the P.T. Badak LNG plant in Bontang, Kalimantan, Indonesia. At that time, I felt the only position that was coming up with Kellogg would have been in a single status situation, so I accepted the offer with Roy M. Huffington as it was family status and would have a school for Tammie who would start her 8th grade in August. I knew the camp facilities very well from my position on that site in 1983, and the school was very good. So, we mobilize in the first week of July of that year to Bontang. The family immediately settled in, and my job went very well, mostly as a rotating equipment supervisor on nine-hour days Monday through Friday, and every other Saturday off. My position was on call for any emergencies, but I rarely had to spend much time outside regular working hours other than scheduled shutdowns. It was the perfect project in our situation with Tammy in the eighth grade. We could have put Richie and Debbie in a private high school in Singapore, but they preferred to continue their high school in Missouri. Rather than rent our house, we arranged for Kim, my niece, and her husband, Lowell Clift, to house sit for us while in Indonesia, and they kept Richie and Debbie, which worked out very well. Lowell and Kim were in their twenties, so they understood the two teenagers and did a great job with the two children.

Tammie had a rough time sometimes when underestimating the sun near the equator. On her first birthday there, when her class went to Wreak Island, Tammie is a redhead and spent too much time in the sun. That is a mistake often made when sunning near the equator, especially fair-skin-complexion people. She was unable to attend school for over a week while suffering through those burns. Her teacher, Mrs. Taylor, made her a special birthday cake with a giant topping décor of Mickey Mouse. When restricted to a camp, even with one of the best, children always found a reason to have a party, and these expat children formed bonds during their time in these camps that continue throughout their lives. Each time we visited the village, the young children would run up to her just to touch her hair, a little scary for Tammie at first, but she got accustomed to it very quickly.

We were provided with a very nice furnished three-bedroom house. I knew several of the staff from other projects and a few I had met a year earlier. We had a very good social life and all the amenities that came with the job. The family enjoyed many weekends on a couple of small islands off the coast of Bontang in the Sulawesi Sea. There were several boats we could use with a local driver to take us to either of these islands. The largest of those was set up where families of the P.T. Badak employees could take their children and have a safe day at the beach and do some beautiful snorkeling just offshore from the beach. We, like all expats, enjoyed finding beautiful shells and watching all the sea life. Our favored boat driver was a special character whose American name was Tequila. The sea was basically a safe place for children other than a few stingrays a person could step on and might cause a painful sting. We all wore special beach shoes that provided good protection. However, on one outing to Sand Island, Tammie stepped on one of those stingrays that stung her foot just above the shoes. Tequila grabbed her and immediately cut her foot with his pocketknife at the spot where she was stung, making a cut, and then began sucking out as much blood as he could very quickly. We took her into the camp hospital to get her treated and do something to relieve the pain. The local doctor told us she was lucky that Tequila immediately did what he did to keep the poison from making it worse. She had some pain for a couple hours, but it took a couple weeks to heal.

Before we mobilized, I bought a nice fishing reel and tackle to suit fishing in the sea. I, along with many of the expats there, would often take a boat out on weekends and fish. We normally would catch nice fish such as grouper, red snapper, and several other types of fish. The locals also fished on their days off, but they preferred to use handheld hand lines while fishing. One Saturday, as I was working my weekend schedule, a phone call came into our maintenance office, it was from the boat dock asking for a fifteen-ton rubber tire crane; we call them "cherry pickers." After some time being confused about why they wanted that cherry picker, our crane driver drove down to the dock. When he arrived, he found those locals had a large swordfish tied to the side of their boat. We learned they caught the fish on their handheld line with a one-hundred-pound line; the fish pulled the boat around until the fish finally got tired and the fisherman tied the fish to the boat. After a couple of hours, the fish finally became tired, and the fishermen pulled the fish up against the boat and tied it where it couldn't get loose. We have always heard the old saying, "the big one got away," so I am including an old photo after the fish had been pulled out of the water. This one didn't get away.

None of us Expats with our nice reels and tackles had ever caught anything like this one. It weighed over five hundred pounds. It was donated to the local orphanage in Bontang.

The first weekend there in Bontang, I rejoined the Hash House Harriers and was welcomed back. When you run your first race, you get initiated into the Harriers and given a name. I received the name "Shockabsorber" and then all the Harriers sang the following song.

"¶Here's to Shockabsorber; he's true blue,
He's a bastard through and through,
He's not going to heaven; he went the other way!
Drink it down, down, down, down……¶"

Then you had to drink beer from a mug full in one go, and then you received your name and became a Hash House Harrier. I ran over fifty races and received the Hash House Harrier pewter cup. During my time spent in Bontang, after I became a regular, I occasionally laid out the trails a day prior to a race. Of all the races I was involved in, we never had a snake bite or had any wild animals chasing us other than a couple of water buffalo who felt their babies were threatened. Hash House Harriers have nothing to do with hash.

Each year on a certain holiday, P.T. Badak sponsored a ten-mile run on a dirt road called "the equator road" or sometimes called "the pipeline road" that crossed the equator. Tt was a maintenance road for one of the gas pipelines that ran from a gas well to the LNG plant. Our project had two engineers who had run cross-country in college competitions. On the first day I ran the race, one of these engineers did all his proper exercise while a small Indonesian stood by smoking a couple of his Kretek cigarettes. These are special to that part of the world. They have cloves mixed with tobacco and smell like cloves. The little Indonesian ran alongside the engineer and talked for nine miles, then took off leaving everyone behind including the engineer and won the race. When the engineer got to the finish line the Indonesian was smoking his Kretek cigarettes. Of course, I, not being a very good runner, came in somewhere in the middle of the pack.

Living in the camp was like living in a very nice neighborhood where everyone knew one another, but we didn't have to mow the lawn or fix anything around the house when something broke down; we just had to call the maintenance department. We lived in great surroundings with our house at the edge of the camp with the jungle starting about one hundred feet from our house. However, it was safe enough to walk inside the fence of the camp at any time of the day or night. Every day when we woke up, we could hear all the animals and birds making their morning noises, and occasionally an orangutan would wander over the fence into the yard. It was still nice sitting on the porch and drinking your coffee before going to work, just listening to nature. There were dangerous animals and snakes in the jungle, but we never had any problem within the camp, and the security was great. Most evenings, there were card games in someone's house or in one of the recreational rooms. I am sure it could get a little boring for a wife who accompanied their husband. Everything was provided, including a full-time maid. But these women could take a couple of short flights a year to Singapore to do some occasional shopping. When one woman found something unusual that might fit in their home in the U.S.A., many of the other women would pick up one of these unusual items on their next trip to Singapore. One item that brings back memories was the copper noodle cart which stood about three feet high and was perfect to be a little bar where you could have your favorite drinks, or with your whisky decanter on display. My wife was no exception; we had a noodle cart that was in the freight home at the end of the job.

There was always a term for the children of expat; they were often referred to as "expat brats." They did have the "life of Riley!" Within the camp, there were movies, game rooms, tennis courts, swimming pools, a nine-hole golf course, and many other things to keep them happy. The school had a budget for a little trip each year. One year, Tammie's age group, consisting of around twenty children, flew to Sulawesi for a few days. Of course, they had the opportunity to tour a Tongkonan house village. Some of them are called Toraja houses, and have a structured saddleback roof with upswept gables, unique to the area. Of course, Tammie had a little cash to buy some novelties, which included a miniature Toraja house that stands about two feet tall and a 24-carat gold bracelet, another item to include in the freight home. I think that just about defines an expat brat. To be fair, Tammie was always respectful and considerate, and she gave most of her gifts to family members.

After six months, we had earned rest and relaxation leave for seven days within a certain area of Bontang with flights, hotels, and an allowance for the family. It happened to be when the when Debbie and Rich came over for a three-month school holiday. So, we chose the beautiful Kuta Beach in Bali. Rather than a hotel, we chose a very nice three-bedroom bungalow with a thatched roof about fifty feet from the beach. We also took a private bus tour through the beautiful, terraced mountain rice fields on our way to a special temple in the mountains with monkeys crawling all over the structure begging for us tourists to throw them some food. We also had one teenager who was in love with a boy back in the United States. Rather than enjoying the beach and seeing the sights, she wanted to stay in her room bored, and thinking of her boyfriend. I will not give her name, but we call her Debbie for short. Bali had little shops with special teakwood carvings, especially along the roadside as we travel through the mountains. We bought our share of carvings that seems to fit well now in a basement box since leaving the project. One thing the family enjoyed was a daily becak taxi ride to downtown Denpasar for some street food or a local restaurant

In early March 1985, I received an offer from Kellogg for a mechanical representative position on a LNG terminal in Zeebrugge, Belgium, that was expected to be a twenty-month project. After some consideration, especially since Tammie would be starting her freshman year in the fall and Richie would be a senior, we felt it better to accept the position. I gave my months' notice to Roy M. Huffington, and we mobilized to our home in Missouri where Kim and Lowell were ready to have their own home.

TRINIDAD

AMMONIA PLANTS POINT LISAS

TRINIDAD CARNIVAL

TRINIDAD COCOA TRADITIONAL PROCESS & DANCE

EXPAT CHILDREN

TRINIDAD BEACHES

INDONESIA

CHAPTER 5 - LOCAL FISHERMAN
HANDLINE 500 POUNDS CATCH

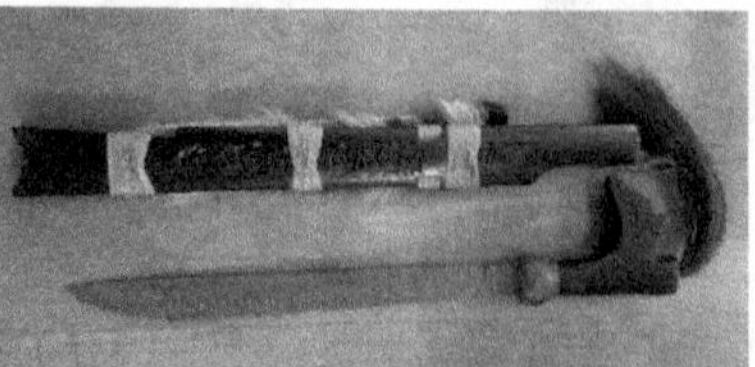

DAYAK PARAN LATOK SWORD

BORNEO BLOW GUN

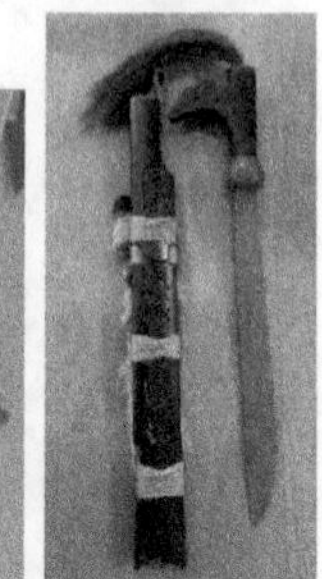

DAYAK SWORD

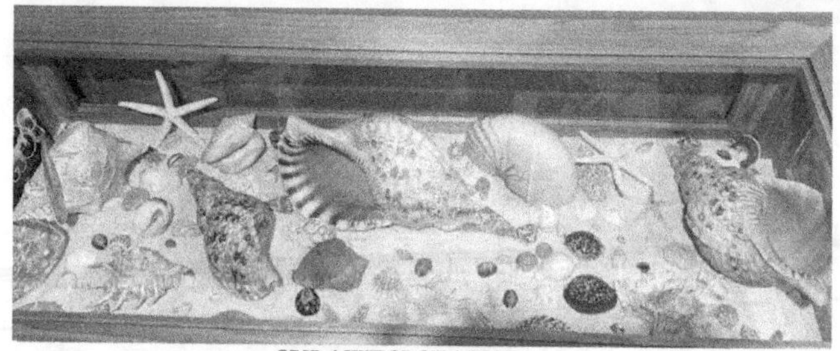

SULAWESI SEASHELLS

NOODLE CART

DAY AT THE EQUATOR

TORAJA HOUSE

VENEZUELA

LAMA RUGS FROM CHILI

WARAO INDIAN VILLIAGE
CHILDREN NEAR ANGLE
FALLS ON THE STAND

CACAPA / ARAPA
ROADSIDE
CARONI RIVER

POTTERY ARTIFACT PIECE FROM
ORINOCO RIVER BURIAL SITE

DIAMOND SARUCA
SCREENS

VENEZUELA BOXITE PROJECT

AUSTRALIA

AUSTRLIAN FISHING

WHITNELL BAY BEACH
RICH, HANNE, AND BEN

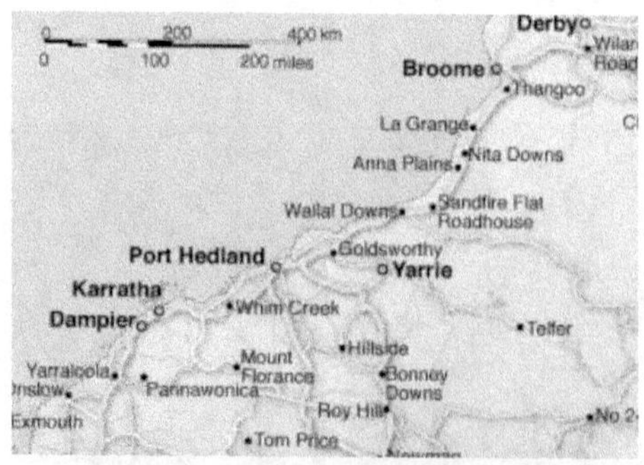

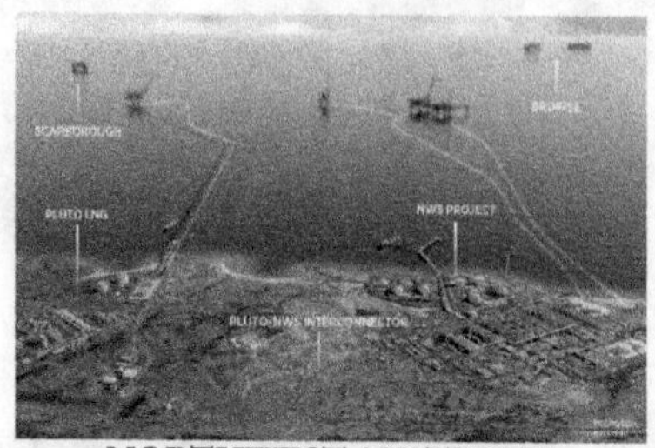

NORTHWEST AUSTRALIA
NORTHWEST SHELF LNG PROJECT

PPS PERIOD

PPS DIRECTORS MEETING SINGAPORE

ZEEBRUGGE OFFICE

MILLWRIGHT DAYS

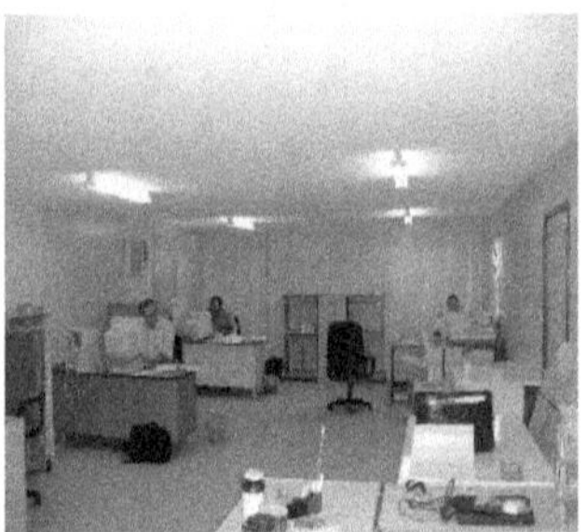

PPS QATAR MANUAL DEVELOPMENT

PPS NIG GUEST HOUSE

PPS CYPRUS MEETING

PPS UK OFFICE

NIGERIA

**PPS NIGERIA
PORT HARCOURT FACILITIES**

**COMPETANCY ACCEPTANCE
TRAINING CENTER (CATC)**

CATC TRAINING CENTER

NLNG BONNY ISLAND

SOKU GAS SUPPLY PROJECT

EXPAT BRATS

EXPAT BRATS is a term used to describe the children of expartaites working in a foreign country, mostly living in camps. I would like to confirm at no times were my children considered "Brats." They were always behaved well, I guess there were a few exceptions, maybe if you will ask them they might have a story or two I don't know. Well, Debbie might have been considered a "Brat" once in a while.

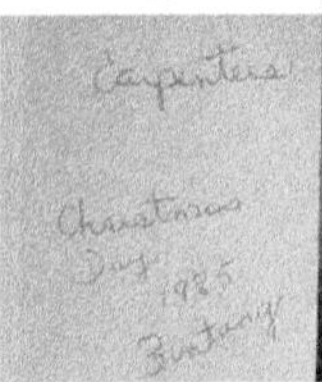

CHAPTER 6

ZEEBRUGGE

In mid-April 1985, I mobilized to Belgium. The contract was married status, but we treated it as a semi-married status with my wife remaining in Missouri to keep the children in school with the occasional visit to Belgium. During the summer months, Tammie spent her school vacation in Belgium and Richie about a month. This was their first visit to Europe, so we took the opportunity to visit in different parts of Europe close to Belgium on holidays and weekends. We made trips to Paris, Germany, the Netherlands, and different parts of beautiful Belgium. Belgium offered many historical places a family could enjoy, such as the Battle of the Bulge in Bastogne and all the historical centers of the main cities.

The job went well, and I added more experience to my resume that would benefit me later in my career. Many of the staff from Kellogg were colleagues I had worked with on several other Kellogg projects. In 1985, the LNG industry was still in its early stages, and out of all the LNG plants and receiving terminals, Kellogg held most of the designs. One of the aspects of the job that would serve me well later was that Kellogg was still refining their commissioning and startup of LNG project into standard procedures. I feel I might have been a little part of those developments with rotating and the mechanical equipment of these projects. This was also my first real project where I was not part of construction and totally involved commissioning and startup of projects. Kellogg had a history of construction and start-up of projects from start to finish of various types of projects. In fact, they were probably the leading company at that time completing projects without major problems in the startup phase of a project until it was turned over to the client's personnel. Kellogg was also fortunate to have a client like Distrigaz that had young, well trained and vibrant engineers who would be the operation and maintenance personnel who would run the terminal for many years thereafter.

One incident that occurred during the project that is remembered yearly happened about six thirty P.M. on a Friday evening. I had just arrived home, and my phone rang, I was told a ferryboat, the "Herold of Free Enterprise," had just sunk just a couple hundred meters off the coast and close to the LNG terminal. The eight-deck car and passenger ferry was designed for rapid loading and unloading on the competitive cross-channel route between Zeebrugge and Dover in England. There wasn't anything I could do, but I immediately went back to the terminal. The back-loading door of the ferry where the cars and trucks were loaded had been left open as the ferryboat left the harbor. Of course, water rushed in, and the ferry rolled over with several hundred passengers on board. It was March, and the North Sea water was very cold in March 1987, and a person could only survive for less than thirty minutes. Many people were already in their sleeping cabins and drowning as the ferry rolled over. Others tried to get as high as possible while some others either fell or jumped into the sea. The Zeebrugge coast guard was nearby and came immediately, but it was dark, and they could only locate some of those in the water. Fortunately, the LNG terminal had a camera on the flare stack, which stood about two hundred feet, so control room operators turned the cameras toward the sea and liaised with the coast guard rescuing the people holding on top roof the boat and directing where they saw a person, which saved many people, but still there were one hundred ninety-five passengers and crew who lost their lives.

One personal painful situation that would change in my life during the time in Belgium and leave some painful memories was at that time, our marriage was going through a troubled period. I spent most evenings in my apartment near Brugge reading books. Just prior to arriving in Belgium, I found out about the Penguin books from England. They were a good source for the history of the Middle East and church history, which was one of my passions. During the project, my first wife and I divorced, which made life in a beautiful country difficult especially with the children living in Missouri with a then single mother. A failed marriage, and especially with three children in their high school years, was hard for not only the children but all family members, and it left scars that made a person feel they have failed others in life. I think it was a lesson not learned from the past!

Commissioning of a process plant requires people, even in supervisory positions, to be in good physical condition. Good physical condition is especially important for any inspection exercises required for piping system, vessels, and other equipment. It always involves climbing to certain parts of a plant to make those inspections. I continued jogging, which I started on the Catoosa project. It not only helped me physically, but it also kept that middle-aged weight down, and it was also good mental therapy. My apartment was situated on the outskirts of Brugge in a beautiful area where I could jog safely on bike paths and paths through nature. During my evening runs, I joined a group of runners from Brugge who ran in marathons in Europe. Of course, I would only run parts of their long runs, and it was not easy to keep up with the crowd. During my last year on the Belgian project, there was a half marathon in Knokke, so I decided to take part with a colleague from the project. My colleague and I finished the half marathon and placed somewhere in the last group that day, but we finished it. That was an accomplishment, but it let me know that with my short legs, even half marathons were not for me. It was better for me to just continue my jogging routine. In the last three months of the project, I had an abdominal wall rupture, which led to a hernia. In November of 1987, I had to have surgery to repair the rupture; perhaps the combination of my jogging and the extra activities on the last part of the commissioning and startup period was extreme.

As the project was ending in November 1987, I was offered a position on a two-year large LNG project in Australia. Again, it was married status. I met Christina, my present wife, a few months prior to the end of the project. It left Christina and me in a difficult situation to decide very quickly about our future. Christina had two young children, Hanne, thirteen years old; and Ben, eleven years old; who were in their secondary schools. It would be difficult for either of them to have their education interrupted, and I had to decide for my three children. Debbie had just graduated and began technical school, Richie was in his senior year, and Tammie beginning as a freshman in high school. After discussing and finding a solution for Hanne and Ben, we decided to get married and take the project as married status. Christina's brother and his wife offered to keep her children while we were in Australia and keep the children in school, which was not too far from their house. They lived in Brugge near where both children would go to school.

CHAPTER 7

AUSTRALIA

In mid-January 1988, I mobilized to the Karratha, Australia, LNG site where Woodside Corporation was building two large LNG plants. The project was located about eight hundred miles north of Perth in North-Western Australia. Northwestern Australia's climate is very dry and can have summer temperatures in the mid-forties centigrade. Christina remained in Belgium to help get the children settled in their school routine. She mobilized later February. Life of an expat was something new for Christina, and it was difficult to be away from her children. During the project, Hanne and Ben would spend the summers in Australia, and Christina would travel home in between our rest and relaxation leaves.

My position on the Australian project was the superintendent over all crafts during the commissioning and start-up of two large LNG plants, storage, and loading facilities. I didn't realize it then, but it was good experience for the future. At times, I felt the position required more technical knowledge and experience than I could offer; however, I had several very good engineers working with me, and the project manager was none other than Bill N. He was the project manager I first worked under Bill in Trinidad several years before, and he somehow had the ability to get the best out of all his staff. I realized I had to dig deep and do my best. The commissioning management started at 7 a.m., and we would work ten hours. I would get to work one hour early to be sure my plans for the day were in order and ready for the start of the day and then work at least thirty minutes after the scheduled day to know the status of work completed that day and how I would prepare for the next day. The project went very well.

Christina and I were just married about a month before I mobilized to Australia. It was difficult for her to have her children on the other side of the world and getting used to being an expat's wife associated with other expat wives. Shell Oil Corporation was a partner overseeing the project for Woodside, so there were several Dutch families there as well. Woodside had built a subdivision in Karratha to house their employees as well as housing for the Kellogg employee families during the construction and start-up of the project with most expatriate families living around the same area. There were several different nationalities in the subdivision with the wives often having some type of function bringing them all together. Christina had several Dutch-speaking wives to speak to occasionally who helped her get accustomed to a new way of life. However, we mostly kept to ourselves with Saturday afternoon fishing at Whitnell Bay, which was very near the project. Christina loved the sea as she was raised on the coast of the North Sea, so she would sit on a rock and knit while I fished. I am sure it helped her and especially when Ben and Hanne came in the summers where they enjoyed the nearby Dampier Beach. Spending time at the beach or when fishing were relaxing times other than the flies, and at certain times of the year, it became almost unbearable. Many people wore a hat with a string of corks hanging by a string from the rim around the hat. The Aboriginals had their methods; they would place a few dead fish on top of their head to draw the flies away from the rest of their body. At the time we were there, Dampier was a small town with a section of the beach fenced off in the sea where people could enjoy the beach without the threat of sharks.

The area basically had a climate where mankind would have a hard time existing (other than the Aboriginal people) with no air conditioners in homes. There weren't many towns in northwestern Australia that existed after their founding other than a few like Karratha, Port Hedland, Dampier, and Roebourne. A good example of one of those towns abandoned was Cossack, an abandoned ghost town in Western Australia at the mouth of the Harding River. Cossack was established in the late nineteenth century with European settlers looking for a better way of life, followed by others searching for gold, copper, tin, and pearls in the sea. Some communities survived, but Cossack and a few other towns were abandoned after many died from serious illnesses and an unexpectedly hard life. Cossack was one of those towns near Karratha we could visit on a Sunday.

Life for a family was comfortable with plenty of things to do for the two-year period we were there, even with the hot weather, sometimes reaching in the near fifty degrees centigrade (nearly one hundred twenty degrees Fahrenheit). There was a hotel in Karratha that opened its large swimming pool for the community, and shopping was sufficient with a K-Mart that had all a household would need. During the summer period in Europe and USA, that swimming pool and the Dampier caged swimming beach were nice with Hanne, Ben, and Richie when they made their visits. In the summer of 1988, Tammy came for a visit during her school vacation. Richie remained for a few months with the possibility of finding some work before he continued his school in USA. After he found out the difficulties of getting a work permit, he travelled home. Hanne, Ben, Tammie, and Richie got to know one another and made a family bond that has lasted to present day. There was always a function going on that we could get involved in whether it was from Kellogg, Woodside, or some community activity. I continued my daily jogging and even had the opportunity to run in a couple of Hash House Harriers events in Karratha. We did enjoy our yard, even with the flies and heat, with a screened tent set up with a table and chairs. It was also a place Christina and the kids could enjoy early in the mornings and late in the day. One event that golfers sponsored each year was a sand golf tour, where each person had a golf club and their one ball. It was laid-out path through the dry arid land for about a five-mile circle. There wasn't really a winner; it was just a fun day, with many participating in drinking a few of the best Australian beer brands after finishing the tour.

Northwest Australia is mostly unlivable for humans other than the Aboriginals due to the dry, very hot landscape, the example of the Cossacks who tried to set up a settlement in the nineteenth century. On top of these nonliving conditions, there is always a threat of seasonal typhoons coming out of the Indian Ocean. During Christina's mid-year trip home returns from Belgium, a typhoon formed in the northeastern part of the Indian Ocean. She had left Brussels on Garuda Airlines in time to get back to Karratha before the typhoon would strike, but even as she boarded the airplane in Brussels, an announcement stated there were some technical problems and they would have to disembark until the problem was resolved. That took twenty-four hours. Once the airplane took off the next day, the people had to be seated in one area of the airplane until they were at a flying altitude. They had a normal stop in Bahrain, so they were again instructed to disembark for some technical reason to be resolved, which took several hours to fix. Once it took off, they made another landing in Singapore with a similar situation before they could fly on to Sydney and then to Perth before boarding a flight on to Karratha. Yes, it was quite a journey for her only second flight without me with her.

During Christina's five-day flight, the typhoon headed directly towards Port Hedland. We had to carry out a tie-down of the whole project site in preparation for when and if it landed in the site area. Once prepared, the predictions of where it was going to hit at full force, and all the people on site other than essential people were instructed to go home and make total preparations given by the government in the area. It did land, and very high winds lasted for at least four days. I was alone in our house with the windows and walls vibrating and all our trees were either blown over or totally stripped of limbs and leaves. I sat it out with my battery-operated short-wave radio on full time for up-to-date weather reports. There was a lot of damage in the area with minimal damage to our project. Our little car was pushed into the back of the carport destroying the storage part of the carport. It wasn't too serious for us other than that damage, and Christina was finally able to make her way home just as an all clear was announced.

When I look back on my lifetime as an expat, I realize I often selfishly got caught up with my career and drive without the consideration I should have had for my wife and family. However, during our stay in Australia, we were able to enjoy our lives in numerous ways that bring back many good memories. I will end this chapter mainly with some of those activities that bring back good memories of our stay in Australia.

Besides fishing at Whitnell Bay, we often spent a weekend day on other shorelines. There was a beach north of Karratha between Port Hedland and Broome called Eighty Mile Beach. It is a significant natural and cultural landmark. It is the longest uninterrupted beach in western Australia; in fact, it is over one hundred miles long. At the beginning of the stretch out of Port Hedland, we often fished off some rocks that were about six feet above the sea, depending on the tide. Christina sat about fifty feet from the shoreline as a tide could splash over the rocks, but I always stood there even if I got wet occasionally. We normally took one of the Japanese representatives with us as it was a good place to catch cod, good for his sashimi. The problem with taking Sassou, who was in his late sixties, was that he didn't like losing his line if he thought there might also be a codfish on his line. I was afraid he might want to jump in to retrieve what he thought could be a codfish on his line and not get out. The sea was always very rough and full of dangerous snakes and other things, so feeling responsible, I often told Sassou to stay at least six feet from the edge. On one occasion, a huge wave came in and when it drew back, Sassou disappeared in the sea. The only thing I could see was his head and his fishing rod, which he was clinging to, never making any noise or howling for help. Fortunately, a large wave brought him close enough to grab his rod, and I was able to pull him and his fishing line with that codfish he didn't want to lose. He and I were also the first on the job in our office each morning. For about two weeks afterwards, Sassou would come into my office and bow saying, "sorry, so sorry; I shamed myself, I shame myself." Later in life, he never forgot our fishing days and became an important link between my business and the Japan Gas Corporation.
We were able to do some visiting around Australia during

our time off or on our way flying out or back into Australia on our yearly home leave. We did the tourist trip up and down Sydney Harbor and toured the Sydney area on our trip back from home leave and did a two-day wine region tour south of Perth in Margaret area. We also had the opportunity for Christina to fly home for a few weeks and make a return with Hanne and Ben where we met in Singapore on their first trip to Australia. We had a four-day tour of Singapore and then on to Perth. The airlines were very good to look after the two young children when they did fly alone to make sure they caught the right flight and enjoyed first class seats. On that first visit when they arrived, we spent a few days in the Perth area with a tour around the city and Fremantle area, which holds good memories of their visit to Australia. We especially have good memories of a Dutch restaurant in Perth where they sang old Dutch songs that they knew and enjoyed a little dance. Of course, when in the Perth area, a day ferry trip to Rottnest Island for an enjoyable tour of the island was very nice for the family.

The most memorable week of rest and relaxation we had was a trip to Broome from Karratha in our personal car. It is just over five hundred miles between the two towns, and at that time, there was only one gas station in between, so we had to be sure we had emergency supplies of water and other items we might need if our car broke down in between. There was very little traffic during that time other than a few trucks and the occasional Aboriginal person walking in the desolate landscape around that part of northwestern Australia. It always raised the question of where they were going, seemingly just wandering alone in the very hot weather miles from anywhere. One thing for sure, they knew how to survive in extreme weather. The gas station was unique as are most of Australia gas stations in the outback, and we were ready for that stop for a short walk and to relieve ourselves other than on the side of the road. We enjoyed the sites of Broome, the pearl industry, a walk on the coast, and on the main peer of Broome.

The job ended at the middle of December 1989 with no other future project announced, but that was okay by us. We were ready for some time off and had time to prepare for Christmas. The project in Australia might have been difficult for Christina and her children spending times apart, but it also was a great experience for all of us. I had met more colleagues that I would work with many times afterwards.

CHAPTER 8

IRAQ & ANTWERP

After a few weeks home back in Belgium in February 1990, Kellogg asked me to take a short-term project in Iraq near the city of Baiji on an ammonia and urea project, which was in the middle of startup. Baiji is about one hundred thirty miles due north near the Tigris River. The ammonia plant was a Kellogg design built by Hitachi Engineering and Construction Company from Japan and an Italian company. Kellogg had been requested to assist with the startup due to many problems. I was part of a team of start-up engineers to assist with the problems for an expected period of three months. I was acquainted with most of the team members from previous projects including Mr. Chamberlain, who was the project manager on the Venezuelan project where he and I had been on loan from Kellogg seven years earlier. I was one of four mechanical engineers in the team.

In mid-March both the ammonia and urea plants were started up with a few minor problems to correct before a test run and turnover to the client, which could take up to a couple of months under the conditions of the plant. A celebration was held with Saddam Hussein attending, but all expatriates other than the plant operation staff were asked to stay in camp during that day. The Kellogg staff were boarded in the Italian company camp near the project. The past two weeks leading up to the celebration, I was having serious pain in my back and went to the doctor in Tikrit to a hospital about twenty miles south of Baiji. After some checks, it was determined that I had kidney stones and was given some medicine that the doctor thought would easy my pain until I mobilized back to Belgium on a schedule leave in May. I tried to continue, but the pain became more severe, and the doctor advised I should return to Belgium. So, I left the site in mid-April six weeks after being on site to have my kidney stones taken care of. On the flight home, the pain became severe, and I went to one of the toilets and passed some stones. The pain didn't go away, so on arrival, I went to the hospital in Brugge where the doctor determined that I had passed the stones, but I would need some time to know for sure and for the pain to go away.

As I would need to have some time off, the site manager decided I would not have to return. He felt the staff left on site could take care of the remaining problems and test run, so I would remain home until the next project, which was in Belgium. When I left the camp mobilizing back to Belgium, there were many army vehicles traveling south on the main road to Bagdad where I was to fly out. The driver said it was strange and thought the war with Iran might be starting back again. I never thought more about it, and a couple of months later, Iraq invaded Kuwait. The Kellogg staff on site remained there as the Gulf War began. My colleagues who remained were taken underground to a facility where they stayed throughout the war. I always felt those kidney stones probably kept me from going through what my colleagues did during that period. However, those who were still there were treated very well and kept safe until they were mobilized back to their homes.

Finally, I got a project back in Belgium. A Kellogg-designed ethylene plant was being built in Antwerp harbor for Belgian; the Fina Neste company starting in May 1990. Kellogg was asked to carry out the commissioning and startup of the project. My position was as the mechanical superintendent for commissioning activities. The ethylene process was another new experience for me, but I had experience with most of the equipment on the project other than the ethylene millisecond furnaces. Antwerp was an hour drive from our house, so I rented an apartment in Antwerp where I could spend two or three nights a week without driving the distance every day. Most of the Kellogg staff were people I had worked with on previous projects. It was always good to work with a team who had worked together on previous projects. We all knew who was capable of any function that needed to be done, and this made the project go well and enjoyable. However, I was again trying to decide how I could spend more time at home and live a family life. So, one the commissioning managers got the idea that we could startup a company that could provide commissioning and start up as an independent company and we could manage our projects from an office in Belgium. With him being an operational engineer and I being mechanical, we could develop generic commissioning procedures that could be adapted to any project, of course, with a few other discipline engineers such as instrumentation, electrical, safety, etc., who we could hire.

We began to outline services we could provide with procedures and guidelines during my nights staying in my apartment in Antwerp. We knew there was an ammonia plant in construction by a German company about five miles from the Fina Neste ethylene project, so we decided to check if they had any plans for commissioning and startup of their project. We made a presentation and presented it to the project manager, and he liked the idea of an independent company doing startup. After a few meetings, we got a letter of intent, so we started incorporating a company. My part of the ethylene project was coming to an end, so I took an early completion, and we started our company in my apartment. Boy, "if I knew what I know now!" I wonder how many have said that. Anyway, we went through all the procedures to set up the company with each of us investing a certain amount based on what we would need to get the company established, based mainly on the requirements on the "letter of intent." Things were looking good with several engineers ready to work with us. About a month after I resigned from Kellogg, there was a finance meltdown, and our letter of intent was cancelled. The ammonia project was delayed enough that our dream went down the drain. My friend was offered another project with Kellogg, and I would have to either try to go on with the new company or go back to work for Kellogg. So, I foolishly bought my friend out and the company was mine, I had to make it work. However, all was not totally lost for me and our new company. I presented our company with myself as the site management for an ethylene furnace project, which was being built in Antwerp harbor. We were awarded a contract to manage the assembly and commissioning on the construction site for eight furnaces that were being built as modules to be sent by ship, two at a time, to Saudi Arabi ready to connect with minimal commissioning with the site plant. I was the site manager, subcontracted through an English company liaising directly with Mitsui Engineering and Construction Co. of Tokyo. I could work part of the day in my office and about a half day on site. This gave me an opportunity to find new projects during the first nine months working on that project.

Process Plant Services Limited (PPS) officially began in 1991. I sure did not know what I was getting into!

CHAPTER 9

PPS STORY UNTIL RETIREMENT

PPS PROJECT SPECIALISTS LIMITED

"Hindsight is always twenty-twenty!" Since retirement, this quote is almost a daily thought. When I decided to start a company, I thought this would be something I could do that would be good for my family and myself. Now in hindsight I know that was somewhat of a pipe dream. After I took a literature course in college where we had to analyze a short story, I always felt I was a dreamer, like Walter Mitty. Walter's story ends in a brave stance in his imagination in the last dream where he ultimately finds his heroism and inner victory, escaping the mundane reality of his life. After the start and selling of the company after twenty years that had some success, maybe PPS was my last Walter Mitty dream. The following is a synopsis of the PPS company followed by a few typical expatriate stories.

When my partner and I started PPS in 1991, neither of us had any business experience. Nine months after registering the company, I was able to get a manpower contract on a start-up and commissioning of a gas receiving terminal located in Zeebrugge, Belgium, with Statoil of Norway. They immediately needed ten personnel from PPS that had various backgrounds such as mechanical, process, electrical, and instrumentation engineers. I was able to provide them, but then a problem I had not thought through: How was I going to pay for these people? My savings could have taken care of possibly three to four employees but not ten. Fortunately, we had set up our company using a very knowledgeable accountancy firm who gave me advice. The accountant drew up a plan how I could fund my projects with what is termed, "invoice factoring." This is an agreement where my bank could loan me a certain percentage of an invoice so I could pay people on time before the invoice payment reached the bank. This included an agreement with the bank to receive the invoice payment and the company Statoil sending the payment to a special account in the bank where the bank would take the interest amount and deposit the remainder in my account. Invoice factoring was mainly used for funding our projects from that time onward.

PPS was off and running. I was even getting references from Kellogg for commissioning projects they could not handle at times due to a large backlog of contracts. I had been lucky to start with providing manpower only on my first two contracts as all costs, including personnel taxes, were for our client, and calculation for manpower contracts were not difficult. However, some of the new possibilities included costs on PPS, and I had no idea how to calculate quotations for a project. Again, the accountant in Antwerp gave me a lot of advice. He used a blank profit and loss statement and taught me how to fill out costs and percentages using the SuperCalc spreadsheet system, and very soon thereafter, we changed to Excel. This helped me in preparing tender quotations to include cost percentages that would have been a disaster had I not known beforehand. I was fortunate to have an accountant I could discuss the research costs with including different types of taxes from each country where the project was to be carried out that would be imposed and other costs, I had not considered in the past. In the early days of PPS, Christina took a two-year course in hotel management that included bookkeeping, which cut down on costs, as well as developing an efficient accounting system. She liaised with the accountancy firm regularly. She continued with the PPS Belgium office and liaised with the company accountant after PPS established its headquarters in Limassol, Cyprus.

At the beginning of the nineties, there were many new gas and oil projects that required specialized services that were not tied to operating, engineering, or construction companies. It was an opportune time to start PPS, especially since much of my experience was with liquid natural gas (LNG) projects that were being built. With the contacts I had made over the years, and a large database of various disciplines needed for commissioning and start-up services, the company began to have contracts in various parts of the world other than only manpower services. When the second gas project finished in Zeebrugge, I moved two of the engineers from that project to my Zeebrugge office while waiting on an LNG receiving terminal project to begin in Turkey. During a two-month period, these two engineers and I developed generic plant commissioning and start-up procedures and guidelines that could easily be modified to the specific design of most projects. The Turkey LNG project contract included the development of operation, maintenance and commissioning manuals, and commissioning procedures specific to that terminal. This contract, with a French company, was the first of many contracts to come that wasn't considered a manpower supply project. It consisted of twelve start-up engineers for a period of just over one year followed by a short training program for Turkish personnel to operate and maintain the terminal. I appointed a site commissioning manager to oversee the work in coordination with the engineering company that was building the terminal on site with an occasional site visit, which allowed me to promote and provide tender quotations for future projects. This became a common arrangement on future projects from then onwards. I thought that with this type of arrangement from then onwards, I could live a suitable family life. However, it turned out I was constantly traveling to visit a client or an ongoing project, which became the norm until I retired. I was on a runaway train and couldn't jump off.

I learned early in my business dealings to try to "break the ice" when first meeting a client. A good businessman needs mental toughness, and that is something I wasn't born with. Someone once said, "Toughness is a skill. I don't think we are all born tough. You learn toughness through your experience," I am sure I developed some toughness but several times my weakness would show up and my ability to not give up seemed to bring some balance. I didn't have the gift to feel at my ease when first meeting a client. I found out in one of my first meetings with a Japanese delegation arriving in Belgium that sometimes a little joke, common interest such as sports, weather, or something nonpolitical could give me the courage to talk at my ease. The French company that was building ethylene furnaces in Antwerp that was to be shipped to Saudi Arabia for Mitsui Engineering and Construction Corporation from Japan set up a meeting for me with the Japanese management who were arriving at the Brussels airport with five of their engineers. I suggested I could pick them up in a minibus and take them to a hotel in Antwerp, I felt it would be an opportunity to get to know them before my meeting. I picked them up, six in total with the manager sitting in front while I drove them to Antwerp. For the first few miles, no one said anything, and I asked the manager if he had ever been to Antwerp. He said he hadn't but about thirty years earlier his father visited there while serving as a sailor. No one said anything else for a few miles, and I said to him, "you must be careful, you might meet your sister while there." After I said it, I thought that was it, what a stupid remark, and especially when he looked at me with a stern face and said, "a brother?" I just knew I had blown it! Then suddenly, he turned to me and said laughing, "a sister, yes I might meet my sister or brother." That broke the ice and from there on to the hotel, the conversations started. I got the contract and made friends that lasted many years.

The much of the success PPS did have could be credited to my being a former employee of Kellogg Engineering and Construction Company. At any time, I promoted PPS, I mentioned my period with Kellogg, which was one of the top engineering and construction companies worldwide in gas, oil and petrochemical industries. This got me at the door for a meeting most of the time when a company needed the services PPS could provide. I also used the old "name dropping" idea of people who would have been known to a client. Fortunately, my background while working for Kellogg included working alongside of engineers from several Japanese, Korean, French and British companies. An example was making a good friend with Sassou a site representative for Japan Gas Corporation (JGC) engineer in Australia. During my time in Australia, he became my fishing buddy. Several times later when I visited JGC in Japan, Sassou would accompany me to the beginning of the meeting, he was an older employee at that time and had great respect from the persons I would meet during my JGC visits.

Over the lifetime of PPS, until it was sold and no longer required my involvement, PPS had contracts with most of the major international gas and oil operating and engineering companies on most continents. At the height of PPS, we had the head financial office in Limassol, Cyprus, operating offices in five locations, and three training centers. At the time the company was sold, services were marketed as The PPS GROUP as a dedicated service or combination of services a project might require. At the time of the PPS being sold, the client list included most of the major gas and oil operating, engineering and construction companies throughout the world. The following page outlines the five types of specialized services to support gas, oil, and energy projects worldwide.

The PPS GROUP provided the following range of services to the gas, oil, and energy industry worldwide:
        Design / Engineering / Fabrication
        PDF and P&ID Development
        Control & Safety Design & Development
        HAZOP Reviews
        PLC / SCADA Systems

Prefabricated Process Skids

Pre-Commissioning / Commissioning / O&M
Customized Procedures & System Turnover Packages
Computerized Data Management Systems
HSE Implementation

Competence Assessment Training Centers
Dedicated Training Centers
Core Training & Apprenticeship Schemes
Multimedia Techique
In-house Process Training Systems
O&M Operations / I&E / Mechanical Personnel Training

Manpower
Comprehensive Management Database
All Major Disciplines & Specialized Personnel
Vetting Procedures
Recruitment
Medical, Mobilization, and Full Administration

Data Solutions
Computerized Data Management
Tracking & Controlling Pre-Com./ Commissioning
Maintenance Management Procedures & Systems
Automated Stock Control / Job Routines

TYPICAL EXPATRIATE STORIES

The remainder of this chapter includes a few stories and events that are very familiar for an expatriate's life who has lived abroad and regularly travelled for business. These stories, and the book in general, are some records of the lives we lived as a family to be passed down to the children and grandchildren. These stories will help them remember their lives during that period of their lives and to know what I was up to at the times they wondered "Where is he and what is he doing?" I am also sure that some children of expatriates who reads this book can say, "So that is the story of my expat parents," because all expats who want to tell their story can almost change the character names in the book.

Once the company was running, I had to travel often to promote PPS for future projects, so there are a few stories of those trips to mention. One of the first trips was to Stavanger, Norway, to meet with Statoil that had a gas treatment project that required commissioning assistance. I travelled on to the project site in a helicopter for a meeting with the project manager and his staff to make a presentation. I prepared a simple one-page promotional sheet and made copies I handed out to all at the meeting table. I sat with six of the staff waiting for the manager to come in. Once there, he didn't say anything. He just picked up my promotional sheet, folded it into a paper airplane and tossed it into the air, then said, "Tell me what PPS can do." I felt I had wasted my time and effort to travel up for this meeting but went ahead and gave my presentation. His staff asked a few questions, and the only thing the manager said after the meeting was about over, and I had given my quotation was to the contracts manager, "Can you take Mr. Shockley into your office and get the contract ready for signatures?" My confidence was completely torn apart at the beginning of the meeting, but after the contract was signed, I left feeling, "We can do this!" I had the confidence to carry on.

I never felt I had the character to make presentations, and still don't, but for the next twenty years, it was something I had to do many times to small, medium, or at times, with several people in attendance. A few times, we had to deliver our company's presentations at conferences and often with an interpreter, and that isn't easy! On one occasion, at a conference in Singapore, our company, which was considered a provider of "downstream services" and a partner's company a provider of "upstream" services, was being considered for services for a group of companies in China and Southeast Asia. Most of the attendees were Chinese or of Chinese descent, but thankfully, they understood some English. We were just some of the companies being considered. As the manager of the upstream company, a good friend and I were sitting at a table waiting for our turn. He was very restless as he had someone who was to give their presentation who had a flight delay so he would have to make the presentation unprepared, and he also stuttered when talking. After a few minutes, he nudged me and said without stuttering, "Don, I have passion," and I could only say, "yes you do." He was next and gave the best presentation of the day, and I had to follow, that was very difficult for me!

Most of the time, I travelled alone and stayed in hotels. However, there were opportunities when Christina was able to travel. In some of these locations, we were able to combine these trips with a week or two vacations, i.e.., Singapore, Bintang Island, Istanbul in Turkey, Athens in Greece, Limassol in Cyprus, Shenzhen in China, and London in England. On a visit to our Romanian office, Christina and I were invited to spend a weekend camping and staying in a small hotel on the Danube Delta just before it enters the Black Sea with our local partner and his wife. We ate fresh fish caught from the river and had some special prepared caviar. We often travelled together to Preston in England where we had our main operating office for a period of the company, which also gave us the opportunity to visit Hanne at the University of Warwick several times. On three occasions, we travelled together for a week at gas conferences in Vienna in Australia, Perth in Western Australia, and Barcelona in Spain. When travelling alone, I was usually very busy and didn't have time to visit tourist locations, when my meetings were finished, I had to get back to the office and home with follow-up work.

One notable incident during traveling happened on March 20, 1995, after I landed at Narita Airport about thirty miles east of Tokyo around six a.m. I immediately boarded a train to Tokyo Station where I was to be met by a representative from Mitsui Engineering and Construction Co. When the train arrived, people were running and screaming. They were running outside the station, not knowing what was happening, so I did the same. I couldn't find anyone who could speak English, so I immediately found a phone booth to call Mitsui. When they answered, they told me not to go back to the station and stay where I was until someone came to pick me up. When the company arrived, he gave me a hard hat and gloves then he rushed me into a taxi. Then on the way to their headquarters about ten blocks away, he explained the sub-way systems had been attacked with poisonous gas, and many people were dead. Upon arriving at their headquarters, everyone stood outside until an all clear was given. I was never in danger as the attacks were on the subway systems and didn't affect the trains. I was allowed to call Christina so she could hear from me before she would have heard it on breaking news. Fortunately, she hadn't heard, and my meetings were held without interruptions.

With a travelling career, there is always the unexpected. In 1995 we had a project on a refinery in Thailand, and I had to make several trips and on a couple occasions, spend two to three weeks on the project site. Myself and all the PPS staff were staying in a hotel close to the project site, it was also an opportunity to take Christina with me. On one of the visits, I woke up in the night with a severe pain in my right leg and couldn't straighten it out. I thought if I tried to lay down it would go away after a while, so I let my colleagues know I would come to the site once I could get my leg straightened out and some pain relief. The pain got so bad I had our company administrator take me to an emergency care unit in the nearby hospital. Once a doctor checked me out, he said he thought I had a rupture in my back, he suggested to have an MRI done immediately. I reluctantly agreed, as I didn't have any pain in my back, and I was also worried about catching aids in the hospital. It was a time when aids were rampant in Thailand. Once the MRI results came back, he said I would need an operation immediately. I refused due to the fear of aids, but after laying there for five days relieving the pain with strong pain pills, I asked to be transferred back to Belgium. It was a costly mistake even though our insurance covered it. However, due to a nerve in my lower leg being pinched for over ten days when I did get the operation, I ended up with permanent nerve damage in my lower right leg. That should have been "lessons learned," and I did find out later the hospital was considered very safe and one of the best in Thailand.

In September 2007, I was in the Brussels airport waiting to board a flight to Port Harcourt, Nigeria when I received an emergency call from Christina, my sister Pat, had been in a serious accident. We didn't know her condition, we just knew she was in intensive care, and her husband Frank was also injured but not as serious. I immediately cancelled my flight and arranged for someone else to handle my responsibility in Nigeria while away. I caught the first flight to Missouri. When I arrived, I found out Pat was still in intensive care with serious damage to her lower back, and Frank was recovering in hospital. Unfortunately, it left Pat with permanent paralysis from her waist down, which is her condition today. Frank recovered and always took very good care of Pat. The accident occurred with a brake failure while they were on a model-T tour travelling down a mountain road on a corner. The car went over a forty-foot embankment throwing Pat out of the car. Richie, who owned a model-T, was behind them and he called for emergency services. Frank was a best friend of mine since he returned from the navy in the late nineteen fifties. Frank passed away in 2022. Pat continues to live alone with very good care from all three of her daughters and she always has a positive attitude, an inspiration to all of us.

In late January and early February 2011, after most of my involvement with PPS was completed, Christina and I decided to take ten days in Luxor, Egypt to visit the surroundings. After arriving, we spent the next few days visiting the Valley of the Kings, the Temple of Hatshepsut Karnak and Luxor Temples. We were aware of the effects from the Arab Spring in North Africa and the Middle East but never felt there would be any problems around Luxor where we were vacationing. However, after the "Day of Revolt" in Cairo, the unrest spread to all Egyptian cities including Luxor. People were out on the streets with army vehicles monitoring and controlling the crowds in the city. All Tourist were confined to their hotels for the remaining part of our holiday. Fortunately, our hotel was away from the crowds with several facilities for those in the hotel. Our hotel was on the Nile River front with a nice view, but once the rioting began, all the large tour boats parked on the riverbanks, including in front of the hotel. All flights out of Luxor were cancelled for two weeks until few were allowed to get the tourists out of the country. We finally got a flight back to Belgium ten days after our scheduled departure. We were well taken care of, other than the news on English TV, and not being allowed out of the complex, the hotel provided the normal services without interruption. We were just fortunate we had done most of our tours before our hotel was closed with the city under military control.

I often tell my favorite story of my China visits that is about "hotpot," a meal like a stew in a pot with different meats, normally pork or duck. I took our Nigerian partner, Sunday Omueti, to visit the training center in Shekou after our Chinese partners had made a visit to our Nigerian training center. After we had made the training center visit, the Chinese training center manager, Tony, took the three of us to a famous Chinese restaurant in Shekou. Tony suggested "hotpot," and then he asked, if we liked duke. Many of Chinese people take an English nickname to make it easier for us non-multi-lingual speaking Americans. I asked Sunday if he liked duck, and he said "of course," we thought Tony meant duck. During the meal, Tony dipped each of us a bowl, which is tradition for someone hosting a dinner for guests, which was fantastic. After we had eaten a couple servings each, I decided to dip a small serving for each of us. As I sunk the dipper into the hotpot it came up with a backbone, for sure not a backbone of a duck. So, I carefully dipped a small amount into each bowl without the backbone. As we were leaving, I cornered Tony and asked if it was duck, and he said, "yes, it was duke." I then said asked him was it "bow wow, or quack quack?" He said, "bow wow." I left it there and decided not to tell Sunday until later. It is said that in China they always eat anything that will fly, walk, or swim.

In 1997, we formed a partnership with a British company and after two years if was felt there was a conflict of interest. So, we agreed to a friendly separation of partners with one of the owners of the other company, an accountant, selling his shares and buying thirty percent shares in PPS. He lived in Singapore where PPS formed a registered company to handle any projects we had in that region of the world. PPS also agreed to take over a process instrumentation and control engineering company in Malaysia with the manager then holding a percent share of PPS. With this arrangement some of my travelling was minimized but I still averaged flying over one hundred thousand miles per year.

From the start of PPS until present day, my children have made visits to Belgium and Europe. Christina and I made our yearly, and sometimes twice-yearly visits to Missouri for family visits, normally staying with family and sometimes in a hotel. In 2013, Richie built another house northeast of Strafford and had planned to build a thirty-by-foot metal building for his car collection and other hobby things. We decided that it would be a good opportunity to expand that building to a forty by fifty-foot building with the extra space built into a one-bedroom apartment for us and garage for my car when we visited, and possibly later in life as a residence while "staring at the sun."

CHAPTER 10

AFTER RETIREMENT

This is where I jumped off that "run-away train." Once you jump off, it takes some time to get your balance, just lucky I survived the jump! Now I am in the "round-about of life," I now must stay in my lane and as long as I understand the rules, I will make it for another day without a collision until I exist into the sunset.

Everyone has a story to tell, some might seem more exciting, dull, happy, sad, or whatever, but all our stories have a beginning and an end. When it is all over, it matters more if we have left this life, making it a better place for those around us and for those that follow. Anyway, we will be forgotten in a short time just like the ones who did it right or wrong before us. Maybe this story is more than a record of the past for my children and grandchildren, or maybe it is my way of asking forgiveness for all the times when I failed to be the husband, the father, the brother, the friend, or just a friend I should have been. But at the time of finishing this book, I am not wealthy according to what we think is wealth, but I am fortunate to live a comfortable life in a society where we all live a quality life compared to the other ninety percent of the world population.

After the company was sold, I had a couple of years travelling occasionally to finalize the transfer of business to others. The past fifteen years, I have been living in Knokke with my wife and taking the occasional trip somewhere from a few days to a few weeks, or to my hometown in the United States for a few weeks in our apartment set up in my son's property. Christina and I are in good health and are now just using Irving D. Yalom's book title, "staring at the sun." I think I would have to devote a big thanks to Christina for putting up with me knowing I would never jump from that train until I retired, which I know was not easy for her many times. And of course, I must extend that thanks to our children who suffered with a father who was away much of the time when needed most.

A Special Note

I started this book in 2023, and it is now 2026 and ready for publishing. It is now forty-eight years ago when I went abroad for the first time. I am not sure what the future holds at eight-three years old. Metaphorically referring to that "roundabout of life, I feel I am now on the Arch de Triumph roundabout in Paris where there are no lanes, no rules, and twelve roads leading into the roundabout with those entering from one of those roads having the right of way. This must be at least my twelfth time driving in this roundabout, as I have been in Paris many times on business and on personal visits. Getting through this roundabout is always a nightmare. In fact, on one occasion, Jesus from Portugal ran into the side of my car with his old worn-out car he had just driven from Portugal. I am not sure how that car made the journey from Lisbon to Paris. It was my fault even though he ran into the side of my car, and I had to pay for his damage, which could have only improved his car if he replaced that headlight and repaired the little dent. Jesus seemed satisfied, and he even had a smile on his face after I pointed out that both our driver's licenses had the same birthday, December 25. I had better close for now, and concentrate. It seems everyone thinks they have the right way, with no rules, and I just want to get to the other side safely finding my balance.

ABOUT THE AUTHOR

ABOUT THE AUTHOR – Donald D. Shockley is an American who spent over 40 years working in the gas and oil industry. Most of his time was spent on projects in the USA, Asia, Middle East, Europe, South America, Australia, and Africa. From 1991, he worked as a consultant and provider of services to the gas, oil, petrochemical, and power industries throughout the world. He has been a resident of Belgium since 1989. Other books by Donald Shockley include:

OTHER TITLES BY SHOCKLEY

Fertile Crescent Religions – History of Three Great Religions
Letters from Europe – "2000" Years Chistian History
"20ᵗʰ Century Life in Rural America - The Shockley Family Stories"
Chronicles of an Ozark Family – Typical life of Ozarks Pioneers